WALL EFFECTS

WALL EFFECTS

A comprehensive guide to decorating, disguising and transforming your walls

Katie Ebben

Published in 2003 by Conran Octopus Limited
a part of the Octopus Publishing Group
2–4 Heron Quays, London E14 4JP
Visit our website at www.conran-octopus.co.uk
This paperback edition published in 2007

Distributed in the United States and Canada by
Sterling Publishing Co., Inc.,
387 Park Avenue South, New York, NY 10016-8810

British Library Cataloguing-in-Publication Data. A catalogue record for this book is available from the British Library.

Publishing Director: Lorraine Dickey
Creative Director: Leslie Harrington
Designers: Carl Hodson and Lucy Gowans
Senior Editor: Muna Reyal
Project Editor: Emma Clegg
Picture Research: Rachel Davies
Senior Production Controller: Manjit Sihra

Special Photography: Chris Tubbs
Stylist: Sara Emslie
Paint-effect Swatches: Sascha Cohen

ISBN-13: 978-1-84091-488-7
ISBN-10: 1-84091-488-2

Printed in China

introduction

The urge to decorate walls has its beginnings back in the cave paintings of prehistoric man. First discovered in the nineteenth century hidden deep in the hillsides of France and Spain, images of running bulls, bison and scenes of hunting held a spiritual power for the people that created them. It was thought that depicting images of the hunt on walls would lead to success in the actual event. These paintings used a fairly basic palette of rich red-browns and black, all derived from the earth and forming the basis of pigments that are still in use today.

The Greeks and Romans both developed highly sophisticated interiors. The earliest Greek temples were made of stone, with elegant proportions that were both simple and harmonious. The insides were extravagantly decorated, and many of their decorating techniques were derived from the ancient Egyptians. Friezes were created on a stucco base coloured with mineral pigments, with the pattern or images drawn in outline and then filled in with colour. Even today, the murals at the palace at Knossos give an indication of how vibrant the colour was: elaborate friezes depicting scenes such as dolphins

▸ These abstract images depicting scenes of magic-making come from an ancient cave painting now kept at the Vitlycke Museum in Sweden.

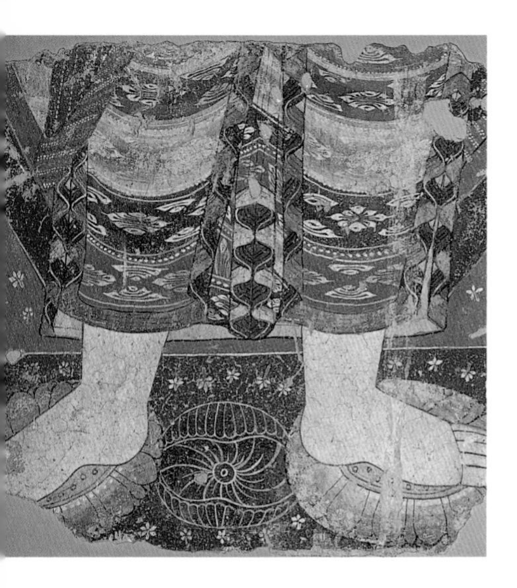

▲ (top) The stucco base has preserved the rich colour of this mural in the throne room at Knossos, Crete.

▲ (above) This fragment of a mural depicting the robe and feet of Bodhisattva, a Sanskrit term for 'enlightened being', dates back to the seventh and eighth centuries. It shows the minute detail used in Indian wall paintings.

and men leaping over bulls are painted with bright blues, strong reds and gold. The effect is graphic and very striking.

The Romans used a decorative fresco technique involving layers of sand-based mortar mixed with marble dust. Coloured pigments were then applied on top of this plaster base while it was still wet. Because of the high lime content in the plaster, the pigments were mixed with a binding medium, probably egg or milk. The beautiful murals at Pompeii depicting allegorical imagery and scenes from everyday life were made using this technique and can still be seen today.

The interior decoration of a home has been used for many centuries to confer status. In the Middle Ages only the wealthiest could afford interiors that were anything other than functional. Medieval interiors were sparsely furnished, but for the wealthy, heavy tapestries could be used as decoration as well as to keep out draughts. Walls were covered with wainscoting or plaster, both of which provided extra insulation. Wainscoting was usually made from oak or elm and, occasionally, painted fir. The finest panelling featured decorative carving with hand-painted roundels, but many walls were simpler, and featured exposed timber frames filled in with either plaster and lath or wattle and daub, finished with a coat of limewash in white or a neutral stone colour. Stencilled motifs were popular and usually consisted of flowers or heraldic images, which were applied over a limewash base using strong colours and gilding. Occasionally, walls would be directly painted with a mural of a hunting scene, providing a less expensive option than tapestry.

During the Renaissance in Italy, the excavation of ancient Roman buildings led to a renewed interest in the classicism of the ancient world. The classical orders of

the Greek and Roman worlds and the decorative motifs associated with them once again proliferated in architecture and design. Popular decorative devices included acanthus leaves, scrolling foliage, paterae (circular or oval ornaments themselves decorated with carving or painting) and swags, applied everywhere, but with a sense of order that created an overall effect of restraint. The Gothic style of the Middle Ages and the heraldic motifs associated with it had not disappeared entirely, but continued to exist side by side with Renaissance classicism.

The Renaissance was also the period of the fresco; from Giotto to the High Renaissance masterpieces of Michelangelo, the technique was widely used and perfected. Using classical proportions as a basis for decoration meant that what is referred to as the tripartite system for dividing walls, with the wainscoting or dado

▲ The rooms of Gothic interiors were simply furnished. The walls, however, were often richly decorated with panelling and ornately carved tracery featuring pointed arches and trilobite forms.

► (overleaf right) Showing rococo decoration at its most extreme, mirrors are used to enhance the effect of the incredibly detailed gilded mouldings designed by P Cuvillies in 1739 for the Schloss Nymphenberg Palace in Munich.

▲ This classically inspired panel is thought to have come from the Nonsuch Palace in Surrey, England. It dates back to the sixteenth century.

▼ During the eighteenth century public rooms in grand buildings such as the Palazzo del Quirinale, Rome, were covered with gilded and painted decoration. Here carved and gilded curlicues form decorative borders around frescoes featuring grotesques and rural scenes.

at the bottom of the wall, a frieze or cornice at the top and a field between the two, was introduced and remained in use right up until the Modern Movement and the International Style of the early twentieth century.

If the frescoes of the Renaissance were inspired by the techniques of the Greeks and Romans, many other paint effects came about as a result of travel. The opening up of the Silk Route, the main trading route between South and Central Asia from ancient times until the Middle Ages, led to a demand for expensive materials that soon outstripped supply. Artists were able to imitate materials such as marble, lapis lazuli and even tortoiseshell, and at a fraction of the cost of the originals. In the late sixteenth century naturalistic marbling techniques were very popular, but were soon joined by a demand for fantastic colour combinations that were enjoyed for their own decorative sake rather than as successful imitations. The taste for extravagant, fanciful ornamentation continued, and reached its zenith in the baroque and rococo styles of the seventeenth and eighteenth centuries, which featured fantastic, often whimsical, motifs and opulent materials.

In Britain, the Georgian period of the eighteenth and early nineteenth centuries saw the development of several architectural styles. In stark contrast to the excesses of the baroque style, early Georgian architecture and interior design was heavily influenced by the republished work of Andrea Palladio, a Renaissance architect whose treatise favoured bold but simple, almost austere, classical Roman design. Interior decoration followed architecture's lead in its more restrained style: full-height panelling was popular up until around 1740, and was often painted in a flat colour, the most common of which was a calm grey-blue and green mix known as 'drab'.

▲ This beautiful and delicately coloured stuccowork is from a room within the Villa Marcello, Veneto, Italy.

When plastered, walls were split by a dado rail and then surmounted by a cornice. The field between dado and cornice was painted or covered with silk damask or brocade; fashionable wallpapers featured stylized naturalistic flowers and foliage. Pillars and pilasters were often installed for decorative rather than structural effect and were complemented by carved wooden or plaster mouldings based on classical designs. Stonework paint effects were also widely used to cover large walls, re-creating the effect of the exterior walls of a grand house or castle.

The architect Robert Adam (1730–1794) pioneered the neo-classical style in Britain, drawing again on the Greek and Roman models and particularly inspired by the remains at Pompeii and Herculaneum, which he visited on his grand tour of Europe. His style of design was both grand and refined, elegantly combining colour and decoration, and interior and exterior. Tripartite walls are typical of the Adam style, and in this reincarnation feature a deep frieze below the cornice, decorated with plaster mouldings of foliage or flowers and stylized seed husks linked together to form swags and chains. Gilded decoration featured in many interiors, with pale green being a popular colour for walls. The overall effect was of a symmetrical, light-filled interior that was highly decorative but without the excessive curlicues and scrolls of the rococo style popular elsewhere in Europe.

The latter part of the Georgian era was dominated by Regency style, which was inspired by French design during the reign of Louis XVI (1754–1793). Ornamentation became more elaborate, and many grand homes had a room devoted to chinoiserie, with hand-painted wallpaper and lacquered furniture from the Orient. Egyptian motifs were used to decorate cornices

▼ Although installed in the first half of the nineteenth century in the Rose room at Grand Duke Nicholas's Palace, St Petersburg, this plaster moulding with its white painted finish has a distinctly modern feel.

▲ The dining room at Osterley Park, West London, is perhaps one of Robert Adam's best-known interiors. He designed every element in the room, from the wall and ceiling panels to the furniture.

and friezes alongside Roman and Greek designs. Walls were painted in strong flat colours, including deep yellow, crimson, emerald green, deep pink, lilac, gold and a vivid blue.

The second half of the nineteenth century saw a reaction against classically inspired design and a revival of the Gothic style in both Britain and the United States. In Britain, the main champions of the Gothic revival were A W N Pugin, who designed the Houses of Parliament in London, William Burgess and Gilbert Scott. Walls were decorated with ornately carved wooden panelling that invariably featured a pointed arch design, stone colours were popular for plaster, and wallpaper designs were usually very geometric and featured stylized flowers and foliage along with heraldic motifs such as coats of arms, fleur-de-lis and bold chevron patterns.

▲ (top) This section of hand-painted wallpaper comes from the red drawing room at the Brighton Pavilion. Chinoserie designs were very popular and this one imitates embossed and gilded leather.

▲ (above) This wallpaper is typical of the stylized naturalistic designs popular in the Arts and Crafts period.

▶ A detailed marquetry panel featuring Italian-style Renaissance architecture decorates the stairs at Eltham Palace in Kent.

But Medieval Gothic was not the only style of the nineteenth century. During the Victorian period, styles were liberally mixed. Following increased trade and the expansion of the British Empire, classical and Gothic designs co-existed with influences from as far afield as China, India, Persia and Africa. While some designers stuck to one coherent style, others opted for a more eclectic mix and combined bright colours and heavy patterns with solid furniture and piles of fabric. Most walls were papered, and if paper wasn't used, decoration was added to flat colour through the use of a stencil above the dado and another below the cornice. In addition to the geometrical, heraldic patterns of the Gothic revival, wallpaper and stencilling included stylized natural forms such as fruit, willow and acanthus leaves or large floral patterns featuring realistic dahlias, hydrangeas, roses and hollyhocks. Hugely popular at the time, today these patterns appear overwhelming, almost claustrophobic to our eyes.

Designers such as William Morris, Philip Webb and social commentator John Ruskin took exception to the excessive decoration and increasing mechanization of their age and introduced the Arts and Crafts style, which championed a re-establishment of traditional materials and practices, using the ideals of the Medieval guild as their model. William Morris's wallpaper designs were particularly fashionable and imagery included animals among stylized foliage with natural flowers such as poppies, daises and jasmine. Arts and Crafts interiors often featured three-quarter height wainscoting in hardwoods such as oak stained a rich, dark colour. Fir and pine were often used as cheaper alternatives to hardwood, painted in ivory, olive green or sage.

▸ (right) An original William Morris honeysuckle design printed on linen decorates the walls of this room at Wrightwick Manor, Wolverhampton.

▸ (opposite above) This classic wallpaper of palm fronds and fruit in an Art Deco style was designed by Henri Clouzot.

▸ (opposite below) Romantic toile designs roller-printed on cotton such as this would have been used both to cover walls and to make drapes.

The Arts and Crafts style gave rise to Art Nouveau, where stylized, free-flowing plant motifs and natural forms came together in a style that seemed to grow organically from its surroundings, rather than be dictated by a classical geometry. Art Nouveau spread across all media, from exterior architecture to jewellery, including metalwork, wallpaper, textiles and furniture. In Britain, Art Nouveau was championed by the department store Liberty in London and Charles Rennie Mackintosh, who applied a more ordered geometry to the style.

The Arts and Crafts style also paved the way for the interior styles of the Edwardian era, which began in 1901 and lasted until around the time of World War I. Although historical revivalism was still popular, rooms began to be stripped back, cleared of their clutter and became even simpler than the pared-down interiors of the Arts and Crafts movement. Oak and walnut were popular materials for panelling, and although paper and stencilled friezes were used below the cornice to add an element of colour, there was noticably less pattern than before. Textured papers such as Anaglypta and Lincrusta became popular as a means of decorating below the dado rail. Popular colours for walls were muted and included off-white, lilac, shades of grey stone, oyster, pale blue and dusty pink.

The interwar years were dominated by Art Deco, originally showcased in the Paris Exhibition of 1925. Art Deco was greatly inspired by the work of artists such as the Fauves and Cubists, and the fantastic costumes of the Ballets Russes. African and Egyptian designs were also incorporated into the style. It was grand and lavish and relied on abstract patterns and unusual colour combinations, such as apricot, eau-de-nil or lilac with black. Art Deco seemed to look forward, not back to historical precedents. It used new materials such as chrome, coloured glass and painted concrete, particularly for public buildings such as the Odeon cinemas.

During the 1950s there was a marked change in the types of homes being built and this led to dramatic shifts in the approach to decorating. Interiors became more open plan, ceilings were lowered and the room divider appeared. The tripartite system of dividing walls was more or less abandoned; it was fashionable to paper one wall with a patterned paper and use a plain or textured paper on the other. Less formal cladding became popular, too, with brick, stone and pine used as an alternative to more formal wall decoration.

The 1960s saw an explosion of colour and unrestrained decoration never experienced before in interior design. The avant-garde work of designers such as Verner Panton utilized plastic to make three-dimensional wall tiles in vivid colours. Pattern was freely

▲ Large-scale naturalistic plant and flower murals adorn the walls of the ladies' powder room at Radio City Music Hall in the Rockerfeller Center, New York. These designs were painted around 1930.

▶ Brown and orange geometric prints and stripes were the reliable staple of 1960s' design.

mixed and matched; large-scale abstract florals and naturally inspired prints co-existed side by side. Woods such as teak and rosewood were in vogue and used for furniture and cladding, along with cork and hessian (burlap) papers. In the 1970s, pattern became even wilder. Inspired by the Psychedelic movement, iridescent colours and foil wallpapers emerged as a modern take on gilding. Alongside the vibrant colour and pattern, walls were painted in shades of deep chocolate and orange, and smoked mirror tiles, bold stripes and rainbow patterns snaked their way across every surface.

The 1980s saw a revival of the paint effect, with sponging, dragging and colourwashing again used to mimic other materials, and stencilling highly popular as a means of adding pattern. Walls were once again divided into three, with traditional floral papers and matching borders making a comeback. The overall look during this period was of an idealized country cottage, which probably fuelled a reaction in the early 1990s and led to the trend for renovating former industrial spaces. The exposed structural beams and raw brick of these interiors signalled a much harsher approach to decorating, and was perhaps the antithesis of the rural idyll of the previous decade.

The late 1990s and the start of the new century have witnessed a return to a more tactile environment. We look for homes that are easy to live in and that help us escape from the rigours of everyday life. Our approach to decorating walls is eclectic and as likely to be inspired by the images and colours of a religious mural seen on holiday in India as by the texture and subtle shading of a piece of stone. Our taste is more elemental and naturally inspired and no longer restrained by the rules of classicism.

recipes & techniques

This section covers the various techniques, new and old, that can be used to achieve different effects on your walls. Each technique is accompanied by a list of tools and materials and a step-by-step method. Many of the techniques are simple to do, while others require more practice. Before starting, it is advisable to experiment with your colours on a scrap piece of card or wood, and allow them to dry completely so you can then make sure that you are happy with them. An easy way to plan a colour scheme is to paint various shades onto sheets of paper and then pin them to the wall. This will allow you to observe how they look under different lighting conditions and at different times of the day.

As with most decorating, preparation is the key to a good finish. Unexciting it may be, but don't skip on the sanding, or that extra layer of undercoat, as it will make all the difference to the finished effect. Try to buy the best materials you can afford. Cheap emulsion is often a false economy because it does not contain as much pigment as better-quality paints, and so you often have to use more than one coat or add a large amount of paint to a glaze to achieve the desired intensity of colour.

Pigment is the most expensive part of a paint, wax or varnish and is what provides the colour. Most of the pigments used now are synthetic and so they tend to be cheaper, longer lasting and more stable than natural pigments, but pigments derived from natural sources such as the earth or plants are also still widely used. If you are mixing your own colours from powder pigments, always wear protective gloves and a mask to avoid inhaling any of the fine powder.

Pigments are mixed with binders to create paints and glazes. Binders tend to dry clear, so will not affect the final colour, but they will determine whether the finish will be shiny or matt, rough or smooth. Binders are usually oil or water-based. Emulsion paint or latex, for example, usually has a water-based acrylic or vinyl binder, while gloss paint has an oil-based binder, which means that brushes have to be cleaned in white spirit rather than water.

In the past, binders were made from animals and plants or they came directly from the earth. Although today synthetic binders are more common and much easier to use, traditional materials are also available and may include such pungent concoctions as rabbitskin glue (traditionally used with gilding), or even milk (known as casein paint). The vibrant tempera paint of the Renaissance, used by painters such as Van Dyck and Holbein, contained egg yolk as the binder. Gum arabic, a thin but strong binder normally used to make watercolour paints, comes from plants, while the earth provides all the materials needed to make plaster finishes and limewashes.

As with paints and pigments, always buy the best quality brushes that you can possibly afford. There is nothing more irritating than finding your cheap brush has shed hairs into the paint finish. Experiment with different painting tools – a feather, a piece of card or even some crumpled plastic can invariably create more interesting effects than a brush. Some of the techniques explained in the following pages do require specialist brushes, and these are always listed in the tools section. Make a point of using the right brush, as you won't achieve the desired effect without the proper tool.

Wallpapering

Hanging wallpaper is one of those jobs that looks considerably harder than it actually is. If you are a complete beginner, avoid expensive mistakes by starting with a cheaper paper with a pattern that is easy to match, such as stripes or an all-over, single motif.

Tools & materials

Pasting table	Bucket for mixing paste
Tape measure	Sheepskin roller
Steel ruler	Paint tray
Scissors	Craft knife
Plumb line	Smoothing brush or soft cloth
Pencil or chalk	Glue syringe (optional)
Wallpaper paste	Seam roller

HOW MANY ROLLS? A simple way to calculate the required number of wallpaper rolls is to measure the perimeter of the room (including doors and windows) and multiply this by the height of the walls. This will give the square metreage of the walls. Divide this by the square metreage of one roll, which should be on the product label. Add at least 10 per cent extra to allow for natural wastage and errors.
For example:
  7m (perimeter) x 2.5m (height) = 17.5sq m
  17.5sq m ÷ 10sq m (sq m per roll) = 1.75sq m + 10 per cent = 2 rolls
Or:
  22ft (perimeter) x 8ft (height) = 176sq ft
  176sq ft ÷ 35sq ft (sq ft per roll) = 5.02sq ft + 10 per cent = 6 rolls

ORDER OF WORK Start in the corner of a room, such as behind a door, to conceal any discrepancy in the pattern match. Alternatively, start in the centre of a wall and work outwards from either side, finishing again in a less noticeable corner.

MEASURING & PASTING Cut lengths of paper to the height of the wall, allowing 10cm (4in) extra at either end. Use a plumb line and a pencil or chalk to mark a straight vertical line against which to hang the first length. Lay the first length on the pasting table, face down, with any overhang all at one end. Mix the wallpaper paste according to the manufacturer's instructions and pour some into the tray. Use the roller to apply paste to the back of the wallpaper, paying particular attention to the edges.

FOLDING A LENGTH OF PASTED PAPER Take one end of the paper and fold it up to the middle, glued side to glued side. Do not crease the fold, but leave it rounded. Do the same with the other end and then fold it in half again. Wallpaper can be left like this for up to fifteen minutes.

HANGING & TRIMMING Position the folded piece of paper by the straight line. Then unfold the top half of the paper and align one of the edges to the pencil or chalk line. Leave a 10cm (4in) overlap onto the cornice or ceiling and start to smooth the paper downwards and sideways, keeping it lined up against the guide line, to stick the paper to the wall. When you reach half way, unfold the bottom half and stick it to the wall as before. The overhang at top and bottom can be trimmed to fit with a pair of scissors (pull the paper away from the wall slightly, trim and then stick down), or by using a sharp knife drawn along a metal edge. Next, smooth out any bubbles or wrinkles using a brush or cloth.

PAPERING CORNERS The simplest way of hanging paper round a corner is to cut the length so that only 1.5cm (¾in) extends round the corner. When you have done this and the length is in position, use a steel ruler and sharp knife to cut the overlap back so that it measures between 3–5mm (¼in). Hang the next length to overlap the little bit of remaining paper, trimming the length vertically to match the pattern repeat.

PAPERING WINDOWS & DOORS Cut the paper with only a 5–7.5cm (2–3in) overlap into the wall space above and below the window or above the door. Paper up to the edges on either side, trimming vertically to match the repeat, and then paper the middle area above and below the window or above the door.

REMOVING BUBBLES If you have a bubble that you can't smooth out, leave the wallpaper to dry completely. Use a glue syringe to pierce a hole in the bubble and inject a couple of drops of wallpaper paste. Carefully smooth the bubble with a brush or cloth.

SEAMS Seams should be hung so that they butt together. In corners where the walls are not square this is not always possible, so you need to overlap them slightly. Never overlap more than 3–5mm (¼in) as this will be too noticeable. To butt seams together, place your hands flat on the paper, slightly away from the edge. Push the paper towards a length of paper already in position, until the edges meet and buckle slightly. Smooth down with a brush or cloth, ensuring they are well stuck. Leave for 10–15 minutes and then use the seam roller to roller up and down so they are completely flat.

PATTERN MATCHING Some patterns are easier to match than others. If you have a long stretch of wall that is uncovered then make sure your pattern match is as perfect as it can be.

DROP REPEAT This is the hardest type of pattern to match and creates considerable wastage. Make sure you take the pattern repeat into account when calculating how much paper you will need.

STRIPES This is one of the simplest designs to match but it is crucial that you start with a perfectly straight length, otherwise the overall effect will be on the slant. Stripes are not a good idea for uneven walls and ceilings as they will emphasize the problem.

OVERALL PATTERN This is the simplest pattern to match and is good for less-than-perfect walls, wobbly skirting (base board) and uneven ceilings. It is a good paper for beginners.

STRAIGHT MATCH This is also simple to match as the pattern is contained within the width of each roll and tends to be on a small scale.

Colourwashing

This technique uses glazes tinted with colour to create a semi-translucent, tinted wash over a coloured base. Use a water-based glaze mixed with emulsion or acrylic paint or an oil-based one mixed with oil-based pigments. Water-based glazes dry more quickly than oil and are easier to clean off brushes, but oil-based glazes are workable for longer. The recipe below is for a water-based glaze mixed with emulsion.

Tools & materials

Coloured matt emulsion basecoat
Contrasting coloured matt emulsion
Acrylic glaze
Containers for mixing paint
Emulsion brush
Hard-bristled emulsion brush
Soft-bristled emulsion brush
Clean rag (optional)

BASECOAT & MIXING COLOURWASH Cover the wall with the emulsion basecoat and allow to dry completely. To make the glaze, mix one part contrasting emulsion to three parts glaze and stir well.

APPLYING GLAZE Using random, loose brushstrokes apply the glaze to the wall with the emulsion brush, working on no more than a square metre at a time. While the glaze is still wet, use the dry, clean, and hard-bristled emulsion brush to work over the glazed surface with random strokes. For a subtler effect go over the surface again, using the soft-bristled emulsion brush and very gentle brushstrokes to soften the marks already made (see Dry Brushing p26).

SOFTENING BRUSHMARKS If you prefer, or want to create a different effect, you can use a clean rag to soften the brushmarks. This will create a slightly less broken effect.

STRENGTHENING COLOUR Leave the wall to dry completely. For denser colour and depth add a second glaze coat following the same brushing techniques.

Rag-Rolling On & Off

This is a good technique to use on less-than-perfect walls. Rag-rolling off involves applying colour and then removing it in patches. Rag-rolling on is applying the colour in patches from the outset. They can be used together to create a softer effect with greater depth. Whatever you use to roll colour on or off, from crumpled paper to a plain cotton cloth, make sure that it is lint-free to avoid having a collection of hairs stuck to the wall.

Tools & materials

Coloured matt emulsion basecoat
Contrasting coloured matt emulsion
Water
Acrylic glaze
Containers for mixing paint
Emulsion brushes
Standard roller and paint tray
Cotton rags (an old teatowel is ideal)

BASECOAT Cover the wall with the emulsion basecoat and allow to dry for at least two hours.

RAGGING OFF You will need equal quantities of contrasting coloured emulsion, acrylic glaze and water. Pour the emulsion into a container and add the acrylic glaze. Next, add the water a little at a time and stir well. Pour half the glaze into another container and put to one side. Apply the glaze to the wall using a roller or paintbrush. Paint only a square metre at a time to ensure the paint doesn't dry before you have time to work on it, and make sure you have evenly covered the basecoat.

Dip a rag into water and wring it out so that it is just damp. Next roll up the rag, fold it in half and then twist to create a fat sausage shape. Holding the twisted rag at either end and working from top to bottom, roll the rag over the glaze. To prevent big, obvious patches of clogged glaze rinse out the rag at regular intervals and re-twist it as explained above. To avoid stripes and uneven patches make sure you overlap when you are rolling, but avoid reworking an area you have already done. Allow to dry for at least two hours.

RAGGING ON Using the glaze you set aside, pour some of it into the roller tray. Soak the cotton cloth in the glaze and wring it out. Re-twist the rag as described above and roll the rag on top of the first glaze coat. Re-soak the rag with glaze when it starts to run out of colour, wringing it out and re-twisting it as above.

If you are working in a warm room, the glaze will dry quickly so it is best to work with another person, one applying the glaze and the other rolling it off.

Dragging

This can create a subtle lined effect or a more obvious corded look, depending on the length of the brush bristles. The options are single-direction dragging with long, sweeping stripes, or crossways dragging for a loose, checked effect. The latter is best for large areas and on imperfect walls, as a single-direction drag will highlight any unevenness. Oil-based glaze is preferable, because water-based acrylic glaze will dry more quickly and not be workable for as long.

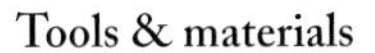

Tools & materials

- Coloured eggshell basecoat
- Oil-based glaze
- Artist's oil colour to tint glaze
- White spirit
- Container for mixing glaze
- Foam roller and paint tray
- Standard paintbrushes
- Dragging brush
- Clear satin oil-based varnish and brush

BASECOAT Paint the surface with the eggshell basecoat and allow to dry completely.

MIXING GLAZE Add the artist's colour to the oil-based glaze and mix to the desired shade. Stir in white spirit, drop by drop, until the glaze has a flowing consistency, slightly thinner than single cream.

APPLYING GLAZE Apply the glaze to the basecoat using a paintbrush or roller. Work up and down and across for even coverage.

DRAGGING Using the dragging brush and starting from the top, drag down the length of the wall in one long, uninterrupted stroke. If one stroke is impossible then brush downward from the top as far as possible and then brush from the bottom upward. Brush out the strokes at the end of each drag so they meet subtly in the middle. If a rougher effect is required then re-brush the stroke.

Wipe the dragging brush on a rag at regular intervals, to keep it clean and prevent clogging. Repeat until the entire surface has been dragged. Allow the glaze to dry and then apply a protective clear satin varnish.

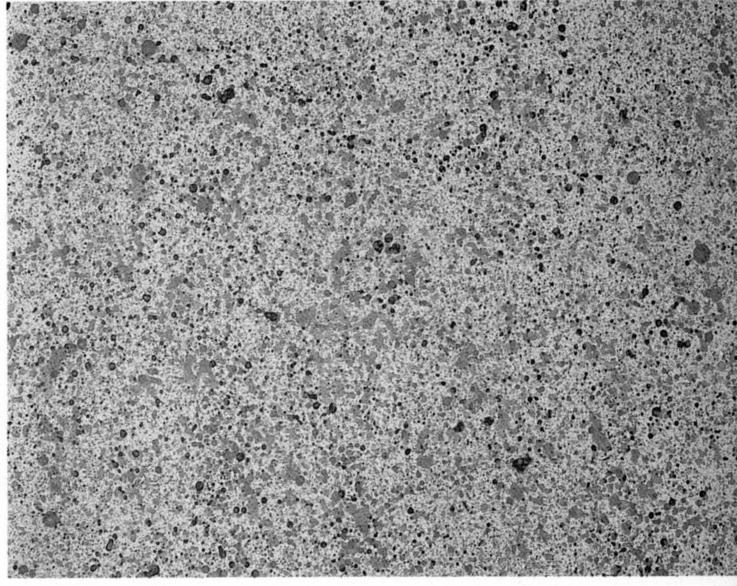

Spattering

This technique works well on small areas of panelling, architectural mouldings and furniture. Beware of using it over an entire wall as it can create a dizzying optical effect if done finely. For large areas, opt for bold, dolloping spatters that create a statement. Experiment with different types of brush: a toothbrush flicked with a stick will give fine, dense drops while a large, soft-haired artist's brush will give larger, less densely packed drops.

Tools & materials

- Coloured matt emulsion basecoat
- Three different shades of matt emulsion for spattering
- Containers for mixing paint
- Water
- Emulsion brush
- 3 x 2.5cm (1in) fitches

BASECOAT Paint the surface with the emulsion brushstrokes and allow to dry completely.

MIXING PAINT Make sure that the floor and any other areas such as skirting boards (baseboards) are well covered and masked off to protect them from paint. Pour a small amount of each of your matt emulsion colours into separate containers and mix in water drop by drop, until the paint is the consistency of single cream. Stir well.

SPATTERING THE FIRST LAYER Stand about 15–20cm (6–8in) away from the surface you want to spatter. Using the darkest colour first, dip one of the fitches into the paint and tap it firmly against the wooden handle of another brush, toward the wall or surface to be spattered. Practise first on a piece of paper so that you can see how much paint you need to load onto the brush for consistent coverage.

SPATTERING THE REMAINING LAYERS Always work from the top to the bottom, using the darkest colour first, and make sure you don't leave any gaps. Repeat the process with the other colours, finishing with the lightest shade of emulsion.

Dry Brushing

This is a simple way of creating a textured effect on a wall. Reminiscent of roughly painted Mediterranean cottages, the effect can also look good used in period townhouses to soften edges and make walls with high ceilings feel less imposing.

Mottling

This technique is often used in conjunction with wood graining. A mottling brush is dragged through a coloured glaze in an arc shape to imitate the sweeping grain found in certain woods.

Tools & materials

Coloured eggshell basecoat
Oil-based glaze
Artist's oil colour to tint glaze
Container for mixing paint
White spirit (optional)
Emulsion brushes
Mottling brush
Badger softener
Rag
Clear satin polyurethane varnish and brush

BASECOAT Paint the surface with the eggshell basecoat and allow to dry completely.

MIXING AND APPLYING GLAZE Mix the oil-based glaze with the artist's oil colour to the desired shade. If the glaze is too thick, add some white spirit, drop by drop, until it is the consistency of single cream. Using an emulsion brush, brush the glaze over the surface in loose, random strokes, working on no more than a square metre at a time so that glaze doesn't dry out before you have time to work on it.

MOTTLING Draw the mottling brush downward in overlapping, continuous stripes. To produce the grained effect, start in one corner and, using the mottling brush, make overlapping arc shapes in the glaze.

SOFTENING Next, use the badger softener to blend the arcs slightly to create a more subtle effect. Gently brush the badger softener from the bottom to the top of the surface, wiping the brush on a rag as it becomes loaded with glaze.

VARNISHING Leave the surface to dry completely and then cover with a coat of polyurethane varnish. Allow to dry completely. Repeat the mottling process to create greater depth, and finish with another coat of varnish.

Tools & materials

White matt emulsion basecoat
Coloured matt emulsion
Acrylic glaze
Water
Container for mixing paint
Emulsion brush
Hard-bristled brush
Wooden board or large artist's palette

BASECOAT Paint the surface with the emulsion basecoat and leave to dry for at least two hours.

MIXING GLAZE Mix one part coloured emulsion to one part acrylic glaze and add a half-part water, drop by drop, stirring well.

DRY BRUSHING Next, dip the tip of the hard-bristled brush into the glaze and blot off the excess on the wooden board or palette. Apply the paint to the walls in short, rapid brushstrokes in all directions. The idea is to keep the brush quite dry to create a textured effect.

When the glaze becomes too light, dip the tip of the brush into the glaze again and blot off before applying to the walls.

DEEPENING THE COLOUR Once the wall is covered, leave it to dry. For a deeper colour, add another layer of glaze using the same technique.

Combing

This technique looks best when confined to small areas, as it needs to be done in one continuous stroke and it is impossible to join lines up and keep them perfectly straight. Try using it on the lower part of a wall between the dado rail and skirting board (base board).

Tools & materials

Matt emulsion basecoat
Darker shade of matt emulsion
Acrylic glaze
Container for mixing paint
Emulsion brush
Rubber or metal comb
Rag

BASECOAT Paint the surface with the emulsion basecoat and leave to dry completely.

GLAZE Mix equal parts of darker matt emulsion and acrylic glaze and paint it evenly over the basecoat.

COMBING If you are covering a large area, work in metre-wide sections but always work from top to bottom. Holding the comb at right angles to the wall and keeping your arm as straight as possible, drag the comb through the glaze from top to bottom in one continuous, straight movement.

CORRECTING MISTAKES Wipe the comb after each drag. Do not double-drag an area as this will remove more glaze and make it look patchy. Also, avoid overlapping drags or stopping halfway through. If you make a mistake, wipe off the glaze with a cloth, repaint the glaze onto the wall and drag with the comb.

DIFFERENT EFFECTS There are a variety of combs available, made from metal or rubber. Metal combs can be harsh on walls and tend to work better on furniture. Experiment with different widths of comb teeth, or even graduated teeth, which are wide at one end and narrow at the other and will create a varied stripe effect.

Flogging

This technique is quite simple but labour intensive, and creates a subtle effect traditionally used for softening the effects of wood graining. It can also be used on walls to give a soft, textured look.

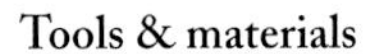

Tools & materials

Matt emulsion basecoat
Darker shade of matt emulsion
Acrylic glaze
Container for mixing paint
Emulsion brush
Flogging brush

BASECOAT Paint the surface with the emulsion basecoat and leave to dry completely.

GLAZE Mix equal parts darker matt emulsion and acrylic glaze and paint it evenly over the basecoat in metre-wide sections at a time. If you paint any more glaze onto the wall it will have dried before you have been able to flog it.

FLOGGING Using a dry flogging brush, tap the surface with the brush sideways on, so that the sides of the bristles make contact with the wall, rather than a stippling action where just the tips of the bristles touch the surface. Move your wrist rather than your whole arm, as this will give a subtler finish.

Sponging

Beloved of the 1980s, sponging can look modern when used with subtle colours that are worked in well to create a mottled, broken-colour effect. Natural sponge creates a less regulated pattern than synthetic sponge – experiment with both to see which finish you prefer.

Tools & materials

Matt emulsion basecoat
Contrasting emulsion
Acrylic glaze
Container for mixing paint
Emulsion brush
Natural sea sponges
Standard roller and paint tray
Scrap paper

BASECOAT Paint the surface with the emulsion basecoat and leave to dry completely.

SPONGING ON Sponging with a tinted glaze creates a more transparent effect than using paint directly on paint, which gives a more opaque finish. Mix equal parts of contrasting emulsion and acrylic glaze in a container and stir well. Dip one of the sponges into clean water and wring until damp.

Pour the glaze into the paint tray and lightly dip in the sponge. Blot the sponge on paper and pat it onto the wall. Take care not to press it hard, as this will create a very harsh effect. Keep the sponge moist, and work one area at a time before moving on to the next area.

SPONGING OFF In this method, the glaze is rolled onto the wall until it completely covers the basecoat. A dry sponge is then dabbed onto the wall to remove the colour rather than to apply it, revealing the base colour underneath and creating the reverse effect to the method above. Both sponging on and sponging off can be used in layers, one over the other, to create a subtle, mottled effect.

Stippling

Although time consuming, stippling creates a very subtle, finely textured finish. It works particularly well on wood panelling and mouldings, using oil-based paints to create an aged effect. The technique can also be done using water-based paints.

Tools & materials

Container for mixing paint
Stippling brush (choose large ones to cover large areas)
Small foam roller for applying glaze
Rolling tray
Rags or kitchen towel

For oil-based stippling

Eggshell basecoat
500ml (1 pint) transparent oil-based glaze
3.5 tbsp artist's oil colour
1tbsp linseed oil
150ml (5fl oz) white spirit
Matt acrylic varnish and brush

For water-based stippling

Matt emulsion basecoat
500ml (1 pint) acrylic glaze
Artist's acrylic paint or different shade of matt emulsion to tint glaze

BASECOAT Paint the surface with either eggshell or matt emulsion and allow to dry completely.

OIL-BASED GLAZE Mix the glaze and artist's oil colour and stir well. Add the linseed oil and about 50ml (2fl oz) of the white spirit and mix together. Still mixing, slowly pour in more white spirit, about 1 tsp at a time, until you have a consistency slightly thinner than single cream. Ensure that the mixture does not become too runny.

Working from top to bottom, left to right and quickly, roller the glaze over the basecoat. To stipple, lightly dab the stippling brush onto the surface in a straight-on action. Wipe the stipple brush clean with a rag at regular intervals so that it does not become blocked.

WATER-BASED GLAZE Mix the acrylic glaze and artist's colour or different shade of emulsion and stir well. Roller glaze onto the wall and stipple as above. Water-based products dry more quickly than oil-based ones, so you will need to work fast. If possible work with two people, allowing one to roller the glaze and the other to stipple.

FOR BOTH METHODS Complete an entire area before stopping. If you are doing several walls, work on opposite walls together and tape off corners of adjoining walls to avoid overlap. Once completely dry apply a coat of appropriate varnish.

Stencilling

This relatively simple method is a good way of introducing patterned elements. There are many pre-cut designs in acetate available, which can be used over and over again. If you are feeling adventurous, you can cut your own stencil using either cardboard sealed with linseed oil or acetate. For best results, cut acetate stencils with a hot cutter; card can be cut with a craft knife. Paint can be applied using a stippling brush or, for a softer effect, a sponge (see opposite page for stippling and sponging techniques). Use stencilling to create all-over patterns, a running border or a single decorative motif.

Tools & materials

Matt emulsion basecoat
Stencil colours in emulsion or artist's acrylic paint
Containers for mixing paint
Emulsion brush
Stencil brushes
Stencil
Low-tack masking tape or repositionable spray adhesive

BASECOAT Paint the surface with the emulsion basecoat and leave to dry completely.

POSITIONING THE STENCIL Check that the tape or adhesive will not remove paint from the wall by testing on a patch first. Position the stencil and stick to the wall using either masking tape or spray adhesive.

LOADING THE BRUSH Decant the first stencil paint into a small jar and dip the tip of the stencil brush into the paint to a depth of 5mm (¼in). Do not overload the brush with paint or it will bleed under the stencil.

STENCILLING Using a light tapping action, stipple paint onto the wall through the cut-out areas of the design. Carefully remove the stencil from the wall and allow the paint to dry for at least 30 minutes before replacing the stencil to do another colour. Work on one colour at a time, moving the stencil along to its next-but-one position to avoid colours bleeding into one another or smudging wet paint.

Reverse Stencilling

Unlike stencilling, this works by sticking templates onto the wall and then painting or sponging over the designs, which are then peeled off to reveal the base colour. This is an easy technique for children to do; they could design the templates and use them to decorate their room.

Tools & materials

Cardboard sealed with linseed oil or acetate for templates
Pencil or felt-tip pen
Craft knife and cutting mat or hot cutter
Repositionable spray adhesive
Matt emulsion
Paintbrush or natural roller

MAKING THE TEMPLATES Draw your chosen motifs onto the card or acetate. Cut them out using a craft knife and cutting mat for card templates and a hot cutter for acetate. Cut out as many motifs as you need to do the pattern. If you want a range of sizes, use a photocopier to enlarge or reduce the motifs, then trace them onto the card or acetate and cut out as before.

PAINTING THE MOTIFS Stick the motifs onto the dry basecoat using repositionable adhesive. Using matt emulsion and a paint technique of your choice (such as sponging or colourwashing), paint over the templates.

REMOVING THE TEMPLATES When the topcoat has dried, carefully remove the templates to reveal the basecoat colour in the shape of your motifs. Colours in similar shades but different tones work well with this technique.

Crackling

This is a traditional technique used for ageing wood and is fairly simple to do. A crackle layer is applied over a basecoat and as it dries and contracts, cracks appear in its surface. A final topcoat in a different colour enhances the effect. Crackle can be used on many surfaces, including wood and plaster. Oil-based crackle varnish is recommended for use on wood, and water-based crackle on plaster.

Tools & materials

Water-based crackle
- Coloured matt emulsion basecoat
- Acrylic crackle varnish
- Contrasting matt emulsion
- 2 x emulsion brushes
- 2.5cm (1in) brush for applying crackle glaze

Oil-based crackle
- Gloss paint basecoat
- Oil-based crackle varnish
- White spirit
- Oil-based glaze
- Artist's oil colour to tint topcoat
- 2 x gloss brushes
- 2.5cm (1in) brush for applying crackle glaze
- Container for mixing paint
- Rags

Water-based crackle

BASECOAT Paint the surface with the emulsion basecoat and leave to dry completely.

APPLYING WATER-BASED CRACKLE Apply a coat of acrylic crackle varnish using the 2.5cm (1in) brush. Brush on horizontally for horizontal cracks and vertically for vertical cracks. For cracks in both directions, paint on two coats, one vertically and one horizontally. The thinner you apply the crackle varnish the more cracks will appear, while a thick coat of varnish will produce fewer, thicker, cracks. Once dry, brush on the topcoat matt emulsion and leave to dry.

Oil-based crackle

BASECOAT Paint the surface with the coloured gloss basecoat: more than one coat may be required. Allow to dry completely.

APPLYING OIL-BASED CRACKLE Use the 2.5cm (1in) brush to apply the oil-based crackle varnish in the same way as above. Allow it to dry until just sticky. Brush on another coat of oil-based crackle varnish in the opposite direction and leave until completely dry.

MIXING AND APPLYING GLAZE Mix equal parts oil-based glaze and white spirit. Add enough artist's oil colour to achieve the depth of colour required. Paint the glaze on top of the oil-based crackle varnish and immediately wipe away with a rag so that the colour is left in the cracks. Change the rag as it becomes saturated with colour.

Marbling

This is one of the hardest effects to do and requires some practice to get it right. Start by looking at examples of real marble and take a photo of a piece to copy. For the most natural-looking results, work within a very narrow range of colours, keeping the tones similar. It is best to use oil-based glazes for this effect, as they will remain workable for longer.

Tools & materials

- Pale grey eggshell basecoat
- Second coat: 125ml (4fl oz) oil-based glaze, 1 tbsp white artist's oil colour, and 60ml (2½fl oz) white spirit
- Third coat: 125ml (4fl oz) oil-based glaze, ½ tbsp white artist's oil colour, 1 tbsp grey artist's oil colour and 60ml (2½fl oz) white spirit
- First veining: 1 tbsp artist's oil colour mixed with ½ tbsp white spirit
- Second veining: 1 tbsp contrasting artist's oil colour mixed with ½ tbsp white spirit
- Containers for mixing colours
- Emulsion brush
- 2 x 2.5cm (1in) brushes
- Badger softener
- Fitch
- Fine artist's brush
- Clear satin oil-based varnish and brush
- French chalk
- Lint-free cloth

INITIAL COATS Paint the surface with the grey eggshell basecoat. Once dry, mix the oil-based glaze with 1 tbsp white artist's colour. Mix in 50ml (2fl oz) of the white spirit a little at a time. Using a 2.5cm (1in) brush paint the remaining white spirit onto the wall in random diagonal strokes, leaving patches of the basecoat showing. Using the badger softener gently brush over the strokes to soften the brushmarks. Use the fitch to spatter the leftover white spirit randomly onto the wall.

THIRD COAT Mix the oil-based glaze with the white and pale grey artist's oil colours and stir well. Gradually mix in 50ml (2fl oz) of white spirit. Apply this glaze coat in random horizontal strokes, covering some of the basecoat that was left showing, but leaving some uncovered. Using the badger softener, gently brush over the strokes and spatter the remaining white spirit over the surface.

VEINING While the glaze is wet, add the veining using the darkest colour first. Mix 1 tbsp artist's oil colour with ½ tbsp white spirit and stir. Using a fine artist's brush, paint thin lines, reminiscent of the veins in real marble. Repeat with the second, lighter, veining colour, applying fewer, smaller veins. Using the badger softener, gently brush over the second set of veins to add a sense of depth. Leave to dry overnight and then protect the surface with a coat of clear satin varnish.

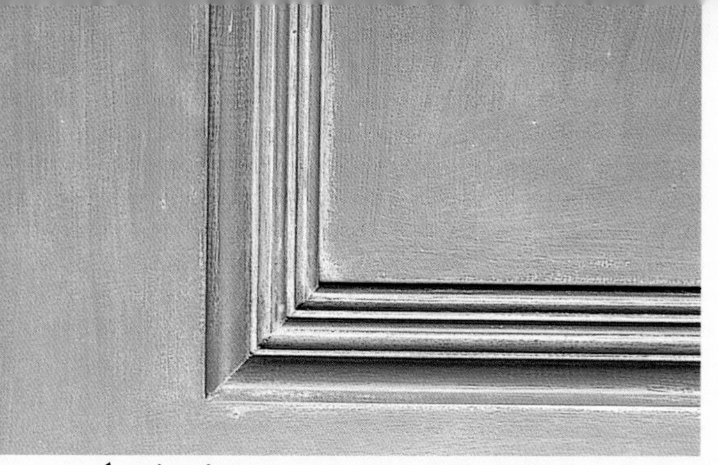

Antiquing

This is used for making walls and wood look old. For mouldings and small areas of panelling that are already stained you can simply rub in an antiquing patina. For walls and larger areas of wood, you will need to make a glaze. Choose your tint carefully to avoid unappealing yellow patches. To create a really aged effect you could distress the surface you are working on (see Distressed Wood p32 and Distressed Plaster p37).

Tools & materials

PVA glue (white glue)
Water
Powdered coloured pigment such as umber and raw sienna
Container for mixing glaze
Large paintbrush
Lint-free cotton rags
Matt acrylic varnish and brush (optional)

MIXING GLAZE Mix one part glue to two parts water, adding the water a little at a time and stirring well after each addition. Add enough powdered pigment to create the desired colour and stir thoroughly. Test-patch a small area to make sure you are happy with the colour, and adjust if necessary. (If the colour is too strong, then dilute the glaze with two parts water and one part PVA glue. If not strong enough, add more pigment.)

APPLYING GLAZE Apply the glaze to the wall or wood in loose, random strokes using the large paintbrush. Work in small one-metre sections at a time so the glaze doesn't dry before you have time to work on it.

RUBBING IN GLAZE Crumple up the lint-free cotton rag so that one side is smooth and use it to rub the glaze into the wood or plaster. As soon as the rag becomes saturated with paint, replace it with a new one to ensure you remove any extra glaze.

FINISHING OFF If you would like a stronger colour then add another coat, rubbing in as above. If you are happy with the effect, leave to dry. If the area receives a lot of wear apply a protective coat of matt acrylic varnish.

Gilding

This process is traditionally applied over gesso, but can look good applied over a coat of red emulsion, which seems to bring out its colour. Dutch metal is a cheap alternative to real gold leaf and is available in a variety of metallics, including copper and aluminium. The gold is stuck to the surface with acrylic size, which is quick and easy to use.

Tools & materials

Deep red matt emulsion basecoat
Acrylic size
Dutch metal leaf
2 x emulsion brushes
2.5cm (1in) soft-bristled brush
Polishing cloths
Shellac varnish and brush

BASECOAT Paint an even coat of red matt emulsion onto the wall or moulding to be gilded and leave to dry.

APPLYING SIZE Stir the acrylic size and paint onto the matt emulsion in a thin, even coat using an emulsion brush. It is important to avoid too many air bubbles in the layer of size, as this will affect how well the gilding sticks. Leave the size to dry for about 20 minutes or until it goes clear and is sticky to touch.

APPLYING GOLD LEAF Place a sheet of card or heavy paper under the area to be gilded so you can catch any gold that drops to the floor. Carefully lift up each leaf using the soft brush and lay it onto the size. Gently pat down and brush any gold that drops off into a dish so that you can use it to fill in patches.

FINISHING OFF Using a polishing cloth, gently rub the gilding to a soft sheen. Do not rub too vigorously or you will remove it. Next, apply a thin layer of shellac varnish. This will bring out the metallic finish and protect it from wear and tear.

Distressed Wood

This is the most simple of techniques, but a highly effective one, and can also be therapeutic after a bad day. The key to its success is knowing when to stop hammering. Once the wood has been distressed it needs to be finished off with an antiquing glaze (see p31). For painted wood you can use wax to create a distressed finish.

Tools & materials

Heavily distressed wood
Hammer
Nail
Craft knife
Painted distressed wood
Wood varnish such as French enamel varnish
Methylated spirit
Matt emulsion basecoat
Beeswax
Contrasting matt emulsion
Water
2 x emulsion brushes
Varnish brush
Small artist's paintbrush
Scraper
Rag

Heavily distressed wood

DISTRESSING Using the hammer and nail, randomly knock holes into the wood to create an effect of woodworm flight holes, which tend to collect in groups. You can also add small knocks with the hammer, but use sparingly to make it look convincing. Use the craft knife to create a few scratches but, again, don't overdo it.

FINISHING OFF Less is more with this technique: avoid uniform patterns or too much distressing, as it will look artificial. To finish off, age the wood with an antiquing glaze (see p31).

Painted distressed wood

SEALING AND BASECOAT Mix one part French enamel varnish with two parts methylated spirits and stir well. Seal the wood with this mixture and leave to dry. Paint the emulsion basecoat over the varnish and leave to dry.

APPLYING BEESWAX Load the artist's paintbrush with the beeswax and smear in streaks onto the wood, following the grain for a more authentic look. Apply the beeswax where the wood would wear naturally and leave to dry for at least 10 hours.

TOPCOAT Mix one part topcoat emulsion with two parts water. Paint over the wood in one even coat and leave to dry.

REVEALING BASECOAT Using the scraper, remove the beeswax to reveal the basecoat. Wipe off any remaining beeswax with a rag.

Wood Graining

The challenge of this technique depends really on the type of wood you want to create. There are many different tools available that can be used to create a wood-grain effect, from rubber rockers to natural bristle mottling brushes and even metal combs. The trick is to study the wood you want to copy and keep referring to a detailed colour picture of it as you work. Try experimenting with completely unnatural colour combinations for a modern, abstract wood-effect.

Tools & materials

Matt emulsion basecoat
Artist's acrylic paint in wood colour to complement basecoat
Acrylic glaze
2 x emulsion brushes
Rubber rock-and-roller grainer
Metal comb
Rag (optional)

BASECOAT To create a basic knotted-wood effect, start by painting the surface with an undercoat of matt emulsion. Choose a shade that is a few tones lighter than the glaze colour and apply it in the direction you have chosen for the wood grain. Leave this to dry completely.

GLAZING Add the artist's acrylic paint to the glaze, drop by drop, until the desired colour is achieved. Paint the acrylic glaze onto the wall in the same direction as the undercoat and, ultimately, the wood grain. Take the rubber rock-and-roller grainer and, holding it so that it is tilted away from you, roll it backwards and forwards to create the knots and wood graining.

COMBING To create a less knotty effect, use a metal comb and draw it along the wall in straight lines with the occasional wiggling action to imitate the movement of the grain. Allow the paint to dry completely. If you make a mistake simply wipe the glaze off with a cloth and start again.

Staining

There are both oil-based and water-based methods for staining wood and the two methods are listed below. The water-based recipe is the easier of the two, but the oil-based finish is much tougher and more practical for areas of high wear.

Tools & materials

Water-based method
Powder pigment or fabric dye
Water
Paintbrush
Matt acrylic varnish and brush

Oil-based method
Beeswax pellets
Bain-marie to melt wax
Wooden spoon
Artist's oil colour
Lint-free cloths
Paintbrush
Clean shoe brush
Matt, satin or gloss acrylic varnish and brush

Water-based method

MIXING PIGMENT Start by mixing the pigment with the water. If you are using powder pigment use two parts pigment to one part water. Fabric dyes are very strong and you will not need much to make a strong colour. Start with 500ml (1 pint) water and tap in the dye a little at a time, testing it on a piece of scrap wood until you have achieved the desired colour.

APPLYING STAIN Using a paintbrush, evenly paint the stain onto the wood. Once dry, protect with a layer of acrylic matt varnish.

Oil-based method

MAKING THE STAIN Melt the beeswax pellets in the bain-marie, stirring them occasionally. When they have melted to a smooth liquid, add the artist's oil colour, stir the mixture, and leave to cool for about 10 minutes.

APPLYING STAIN Use one of the lint-free cloths or a paintbrush to rub the wax into the wood, working it in well. If you are staining a large area, work in small patches about a metre square to ensure even coverage. Leave the wax stain to dry for about 2–3 hours.

FINISHING Using the shoe brush or a clean lint-free cloth, polish up the stained surface to a sheen and then finish off with a matt, satin or gloss acrylic varnish.

Rubbing On & Rubbing Off Wood

This is an effective way of giving wood an aged effect and adding colour at the same time. It works particularly well on panelling, mouldings such as dado rails, and furniture, and is fairly simple to achieve.

Tools & materials

White wood polish
Lint-free cloths
Medium-grade sandpaper
Coloured matt emulsion
Acrylic glaze
Water
Container for mixing glaze
Emulsion brush
Matt acrylic varnish and brush

PREPARATION Apply a thin, even coat of white wood polish with a lint-free cloth, rubbing it in well. Gently rub the entire surface with sandpaper. Do not remove all the polish; you are simply creating a key for the glaze to adhere to.

MIXING & APPLYING GLAZE Mix roughly 500ml (1 pint) coloured emulsion with 2–3 tbsps acrylic glaze and 1 tbsp water and stir well. Paint the glaze onto the wood in a thick, even coat and leave to dry for about 5 minutes or until it is just sticky.

REMOVING GLAZE & FINISHING OFF Using a clean cloth, wipe off as much glaze as you can, leaving a heavy layer of glaze in some areas and a lighter layer in others. Leave to dry completely, then protect the finish with matt acrylic varnish.

VARIATION The glaze can be applied over a painted base rather than straight onto bare wood. First paint the wood with eggshell, sand it back slightly when dry, and then apply the glaze.

Stone Effect

Hallways and bathrooms are good places to simulate stone effects on the walls. Start with a simple sandstone effect that will add soft colour to a room. The recipe below is for an old stone-wall effect. Do this using photographs of a real stone wall so that you can mix your colours accurately.

Tools & materials

White matt emulsion basecoat
Spirit level
Pencil
Ruler
Acrylic glaze that can be mixed with artist's acrylic paints
Yellow ochre, warm light grey, black and white artist's acrylic paints
Water
Containers for mixing paint
Emulsion brush
Natural sponge
Stencil brush
Thin artist's brush
Sheet of acetate
Craft knife and cutting mat
Low-tack spray adhesive
Kitchen paper

PREPARATION Paint the wall with a white matt emulsion basecoat and leave to dry. Using the spirit level, pencil and ruler, draw out stone blocks on the wall to the required size, staggering them evenly.

MIXING & APPLYING BACKGROUND Mix some of the acrylic glaze with the yellow ochre to achieve the desired colour, thinning with a little water if necessary. Sponge the coloured glaze all over the wall (see Sponging p28), leave to dry, repeat and leave to dry again.

PREPARING THE STENCIL Cut a sheet of acetate with one irregular edge to form the edge of the blocks. Using low-tack adhesive, stick the acetate stencil with the irregular edge positioned over the pencil-line edge of a stone block.

STIPPLING Dip the stencil brush into the black paint, and dab off any excess on some kitchen paper. Stipple along the irregular edge of the acetate stencil using a gentle circular action (see Stippling p28) to define the edge of your stone blocks. Add blocks of shading with the grey and repeat until all blocks have been edged on all four sides.

ADDING DETAILS To create the cracks and gaps between the stones, dilute some of the artist's black acrylic and, using a fine brush, paint irregular lines along the edges of the blocks.

ADDING HIGHLIGHTS Use the white paint and the artist's brush to paint fine white lines along the edges of the stone blocks to create the impression of light falling on the wall and give it more depth.

Wood Washing

This is the simplest technique for adding subtle colour to wood. Use on doors and panelling in a bathroom to create a harmonious colour scheme. You can buy ready-mixed wash off the shelf or you can make your own. Whatever you decide to do it is a satisfying way of improving the look of inexpensive wood.

Tools & materials

Coloured matt emulsion
Water
Container to mix wash in
Emulsion brush
Lint-free cloth
Matt acrylic varnish and brush

MIXING & APPLYING THE WASH Mix three parts emulsion to one part water to create a wash. If this still looks a little thick, slowly add more water, 25ml (1fl oz) at a time, until you have a flowing consistency slightly thinner than single cream. Using an emulsion brush, apply the wash to the wood in the direction of the grain and leave to dry for about fifteen minutes.

FINISHING OFF Using the lint-free cloth, wipe the wood to take off any excess wash and to reveal more of the grain. Leave to dry, then protect the surface with a coat of matt acrylic varnish.

Limewashing

Limewash gives surfaces an aged, chalky look and can be used on both wood and walls. It is an easy technique but fairly labour-intensive. Limewash wood using either a paint effect or liming wax: the liming wax method is the traditional one, but takes longer and requires more effort.

Tools & materials

Limewash on walls
Matt emulsion or eggshell basecoat (neutral shades work well)
White vinyl matt emulsion
Methylated spirits
Liming wax (optional)
Emulsion brushes
Clean rags
Polishing cloth (optional)

BASECOAT Apply the basecoat colour to the wall. Use either a matt emulsion or an eggshell paint, depending on the level of sheen you want for the finished wall. It should be a deeper shade than the white topcoat. Leave the wall to dry completely.

TOPCOAT Loosely paint the white emulsion over the basecoat. Aim for a fairly uneven coverage, with the basecoat showing through in patches. Leave to dry for a couple of hours.

FINISHING OFF Dip a rag into methylated spirits and rub it over the wall. Rub firmly for emulsion basecoats and gently for eggshell basecoats. Work some areas more than others to prevent a completely uniform effect. Some of the topcoat will be wiped away, revealing the basecoat in cloudy patches. Leave this to dry for at least four hours. To make the wall look even older, rub a topcoat of liming wax into the surface and then buff up with a soft cloth.

Tools & materials

Painted wood limewash
Stiff wire brush
White matt emulsion
Water
Container for mixing paint
Emulsion brush
Clean rags

Waxed wood limewash
Stiff wire brush
Liming wax
Clean rags

PAINTED WOOD LIMEWASH Rub the wood with a stiff wire brush, following the grain. Dilute equal parts white emulsion with clean water. Paint the wood following the grain. Allow the paint to sink in for a couple of minutes and then wipe with a clean cloth to remove any excess.

WAXED WOOD LIMEWASH Brush the wood with a wire brush, following the direction of the grain. Dab a clean rag into the liming wax and rub it into the wood in a circular motion. When the wax is well rubbed in, use another rag to wipe away any excess and then buff it to a soft sheen.

Whitewashing

Traditional whitewash is a mix of quicklime and size used to freshen up and whiten walls. Limewashing (see following method) is a variation of this technique. Whitewash looks beautiful over freshly plastered walls, giving it a chalky finish while still allowing the warm tones of the plaster to show through. Adding pigment will make it more opaque. You can add strong pigments such as blue to whitewash, but the pigment must be limeproof.

Tools & materials

Lime putty
Water
White powder pigment (suitable for use with lime)
Container for mixing whitewash
Emulsion brush

MIXING THE PIGMENT For every 1 litre (1¾ pints) of lime putty use roughly 2 tbsp pigment. First, mix the pigment with a little water and a drop of lime putty and stir thoroughly. Add the pigment to the rest of the lime putty and stir well. Add more water until the whitewash is the consistency of single cream.

APPLYING THE WHITEWASH Using a clean emulsion brush, wet the plaster wall with either water or a very weak mixture of lime putty and water. Before it dries paint on the whitewash mixture.

For more opaque coverage or more intense colour, apply several layers of whitewash, allowing each to dry and always wetting the wall before applying the next layer.

Rough Plaster

This is a relatively quick and easy technique that works well with many rustic-looking paint effects and is particularly suited to walls that aren't perfectly smooth. Once you have plastered the wall, finish it off with either a colourwash or tinted limewash to emphasize its roughness.

Tools & materials

Multi-finish plaster powder or pre-mixed plaster
Bucket for mixing plaster
Trowel
Decorator's float
PVA glue (white glue) or matt emulsion
Emulsion brush

MIXING PLASTER Start by mixing the plaster according to the manufacturer's instructions.

SPREADING PLASTER Use the trowel to spread the plaster onto the wall. The plaster should be fairly even and not too lumpy, and no more than 5mm (¼in) thick. Work in a metre square area at a time, and work quickly.

WORKING THE SURFACE Use the decorator's float to smooth the surface out a little. Don't overwork the surface, as the finish should be fairly rough.

SEALING THE SURFACE Leave the plaster to dry for at least 48 hours. When completely dry, seal with either PVA glue or matt emulsion, diluted roughly two parts water to one part glue or paint.

Polished Plaster

This technique requires a lot of hard work and effort so restrict it to small areas such as alcoves or plaster panels within mouldings. It can look great left in its raw state, but for a more durable finish it is best to use a colour glaze to protect the surface.

Tools & materials

Multi-finish plaster powder or pre-mixed plaster
Bucket for mixing plaster
Trowel
Natural sponge
Decorator's float
PVA glue (white glue) or matt emulsion (optional)
Emulsion brush (optional)
Clear wax (optional)
Electric polisher (optional)

MIXING & APPLYING PLASTER Mix the plaster according to the manufacturer's instructions and use a trowel to apply a thin, even layer less than 5mm (¼in) thick onto the wall.

SPONGING Sponge the wet plaster with the natural sponge (see Sponging p28).

SKIMMING While the plaster is still wet, use the decorator's float to skim over the walls. You may want to dip it in a bucket of water to keep it clean. Do not apply pressure while doing this – the idea is just to smooth out the surface a little. Leave the plaster to dry for at least 12 hours.

POLISHING THE SURFACE To polish the surface, rub the float on the plaster in a circular motion.

SEALING & FINISHING The same as with rough plaster, seal the surface with PVA or matt emulsion diluted with two parts water to one part PVA or emulsion. Or, cover the wall with a coat of clear wax and buff the wall up to a high sheen with an electric polisher.

Rubbed-Back Plaster

This technique produces a similar effect to limewashing but is much subtler and is a good way of making walls look timeworn. Use soft pastel colours such as creamy white on a yellow base or a soft grey on pure white for a mellow, country feel.

Tools & materials

- White matt emulsion basecoat
- Second coat: coloured matt emulsion such as soft yellow
- Third coat: contrasting coloured matt emulsion such as creamy white
- Whiting or chalk powder
- Containers for mixing paint
- 2 x hard-bristled emulsion brushes
- Emulsion brush
- Medium-grade sandpaper
- Clear matt acrylic varnish and brush (optional)

BASECOAT Paint the surface with the white matt emulsion and leave it to dry for at least two hours.

MIXING THE SECOND COAT For the second coat, mix the coloured matt emulsion with the whiting or chalk powder. For every 250ml (½ pint) of emulsion add 100g (4oz) whiting or chalk powder. For every 250ml (½ pint) of paint add 125ml (4fl oz) of water, mixed in a drop at a time. Stir well.

APPLYING THE SECOND COAT Using a hard-bristled brush, paint the mixed colour onto the basecoat in loose, random strokes. Leave to dry for at least two hours. Using the sandpaper, gently rub over the painted surface to reveal some of the basecoat.

THIRD COAT Mix the second colour with the chalk powder or whiting or as described above and paint onto the wall in loose, random strokes. Allow to dry for at least two hours.

FINISHING Use the medium-grade sandpaper to sand the entire wall to reveal some of the basecoat and the second colour coat. In areas of high wear, protect the wall with a coat of clear matt acrylic varnish.

Distressed Plaster

This is one of the more dramatic plastering techniques. If you want to create a backdrop of faded grandeur – in the style of the peeling, distressed walls of Havana – then this is the perfect effect to use. If your plaster walls are already in need of repair and the surfaces don't need working into to give them a distressed quality, then you can miss out the first steps and follow the final staining step.

Tools & materials

- Matt emulsion basecoat in colour of your choice
- PVA glue (white glue)
- Water
- Clear furniture wax
- Multi-finish plaster
- Powdered pigment
- Containers for mixing plaster, sealant and stain
- Standard roller and tray
- Emulsion brushes
- Decorator's float
- Hammer
- Scraper
- Medium-grade sandpaper
- Clean rags

BASECOAT Using the roller, paint the surface with the matt emulsion and leave to dry.

SEALING BASECOAT Mix 1 litre (2 pints) PVA glue with 750ml (1½ pints) water and stir well. Paint this on top of the basecoat to seal it and leave to dry.

APPLYING WAX Using an emulsion brush, brush the furniture wax onto the wall in the areas that you want to distress. The wax forms a resistant coat that allows you remove plaster and create the distressed effect. Remember where these patches are so that when it comes to removing the plaster you are working in the right area.

PLASTERING Mix the plaster according to the manufacturer's instructions and, using the decorator's float, smooth over the wall in a thin, even coat about 3mm (¼ in) thick, applied in an arc-shape. Dip the float into water and smooth over any bumps. Leave the plaster to dry for a whole day.

REMOVING PLASTER Gently tap the plaster from the waxed areas with the hammer so that the plaster cracks. Use the scraper to remove it.

RUBBING DOWN Rub over the distressed areas and edges of broken plaster with the medium-grade sandpaper. Dust down with the rags.

STAINING Make a coloured stain using 125ml (4fl oz) PVA glue mixed with 150g (5oz) powdered pigment and no more than 50ml (2fl oz) water. Mix it well to make sure there are no lumps and loosely brush onto the wall with an emulsion brush. Leave to dry completely.

Mock Plaster

This is the technique to use if you want to recreate the chalky but saturated colour effects often seen in Mediterranean homes. Mock plaster works well with a large range of colours from bright fuchsia to pale stone. It is also a very durable effect and is perfect for use in bathrooms, kitchens and anywhere else a tough surface is required.

Tools & materials

White matt emulsion basecoat
White wax
Powdered pigment
Whiting or chalk powder
Emulsion brush
Clean rags
Container for mixing pigment and whiting
Protective mask and gloves
Matt acrylic varnish and brush (optional)

BASECOAT Paint the surface with the white matt emulsion and leave it to dry for at least two hours. Using a clean rag and working in a circular motion, rub a thick, even layer of white wax over the entire surface of the wall.

MIXING PIGMENT In a container, mix together equal quantities of powdered pigment and whiting or chalk powder. Wear a mask and gloves throughout this project to avoid inhaling any of the dust or staining your hands.

APPLYING COLOUR With a clean rag, rub the pigment mixture into the wall in a downward sweeping action. Don't try for even coverage; the colour is meant to be uneven and patchy. Leave to dry.

VARNISHING For an extremely durable finish, apply a coat of matt acrylic varnish.

Fresco Effect

Fresco is a decorative technique that was used extensively during the Renaissance and involves applying colour to several layers of wet plaster. Our method creates the colour depth of true fresco but is a cheat's version that is much quicker and simpler to do.

Tools & materials

Coloured or white matt emulsion basecoat
Coloured matt emulsion
Acrylic glaze
Containers for mixing paint
Liming wax
Whiting or chalk powder
Emulsion brushes
Hard-bristled brush
Soft-haired dusting brush
Clean rags
Medium-grade sandpaper

BASECOAT Using the emulsion brush, paint the matt emulsion onto the wall in loose strokes, so the colour is patchy and uneven.

GLAZE Mix equal parts of coloured matt emulsion and acrylic glaze and stir well. Paint onto the walls using the hard-bristled brush in loose, random strokes.

DISTRESSING THE GLAZE Soak a clean rag in water and wring it out until it is just damp. Rub the glaze coat into the wall using a circular rubbing action to avoid creating obvious stripes. Again, avoid creating an even effect.

FINISHING Distress the wall by rubbing in patches with the medium-grade sandpaper. Use a rag to rub liming wax into patches that haven't been sanded to give a clouded effect. Finish off by brushing whiting into the waxed areas using a soft-haired dusting brush.

Moiré Silk Effect

Moiré is a water-patterned effect found in thick silks and taffeta. This paint technique was invented to emulate luxurious silk-lined walls and can be easily achieved with a little practice.

Tools & materials

Coloured eggshell basecoat
Oil-based glaze
Zinc-white artist's oil colour
White spirit (optional)
Container for mixing glaze
Emulsion brush
Wide, flat brush or badger softener
Rubber rock-and-roller grainer
Satin acrylic varnish and brush (optional)

BASECOAT Paint the wall with a smooth, even coat of coloured eggshell and leave to dry.

GLAZE Mix the oil-based glaze with the zinc-white artist's oil colour, using approximately 500ml (1 pint) to 5 tbsp artist's oil. Stir well. If it is too thick, add a drop of white spirit.

APPLYING GLAZE Working in metre-wide sections at a time, paint the glaze onto the wall in vertical stripes. Drag the rubber rock-and-roller grainer up and down the glaze in vertical stripes, rolling it and rocking it from side to side at the same time. Avoid going over the same stripe again. If you make a mistake, brush out the marks and start again.

SOFTENING THE EFFECT Using a wide, flat brush or badger softener, gently brush over the marks to soften them. Continue until there are no harsh lines and the wall has a soft, slightly blurred look.

PROTECTING Leave to dry. The wall can be protected with a coat of satin acrylic varnish if necessary.

Silk Paper

This uses very similar techniques to decoupage, but achieves its effect through texture rather than pattern. It is a good way of disguising less-than-perfect walls. This method uses sheets of silk paper to cover the walls, creating a subtly veined and crumpled surface. Other types of paper can be used as long as they are thin – otherwise the finished effect will not be as subtle.

Tools & materials

Sheets of silk paper
Fabric dye
Container for mixing dye
PVA glue (white glue)
Acrylic glaze
Artist's acrylic colour to tint glaze
Flat brush
Emulsion brush
Foam roller

DYEING THE PAPER Dilute the fabric dye to make a subtle wash and paint it onto each sheet of silk paper with a flat brush. While the sheets are still wet, crumple them into little balls and then smooth out. This will force the dye into the creases and will create a thread-vein effect. Allow to dry.

APPLYING THE GLUE Using the emulsion brush, paint the PVA glue onto the wall and then roller it out with the foam roller to a smooth, even layer. Work in metre-square patches so the glue doesn't dry out before you hang the paper.

APPLYING THE PAPER Press the silk paper sheets flat onto the wall, with the coloured side facing the wall. Smooth out any air bubbles. Repeat the process until the wall is covered.

PROTECTIVE VARNISH When the paper is dry, mix equal parts PVA glue and water and, using the sheepskin roller, cover the surface to form a protective coat.

VARIATION If you want to add more colour to the wall you could finish it off with an antiquing glaze (see p31) or an antiquing patina (see Decoupage p40).

Decoupage

Decoupage, the technique of gluing old prints and photographs onto a surface, was originally used in place of framed pictures and expensive wallpaper. It is a simple and effective way to add pattern to a wall. Old ornamental pattern and botanical print books are good sources of images.

Tools & materials

Photocopies of images in various sizes
Satin or matt acrylic varnish and flat brush
Scissors
PVA glue (white glue)
Emulsion brush
Wallpapering brush (optional)
Artist's brush
Antiquing patina
Rags

SEALING THE IMAGES Seal the ink in the photocopied images with a coat of acrylic varnish and a flat brush. Leave to dry.

GLUING THE IMAGES Cut out the images and then paste the reverse with a coat of PVA glue. Position the images on the wall, smoothing out any air bubbles. You can use a wallpapering smoothing brush for this stage if you find it easier. Repeat until all the images are in position and leave to dry.

ANTIQUING PATINA Apply a small amount of the antiquing patina over each design, using the artist's brush. Paint the images one at a time so you can work the patina before it dries. Next, use a rag to rub the patina over the design and surrounding area, spreading it out to create a patchy, cloudy look. Repeat the process until all the images and the wall have a light covering of antiquing patina.

SEALING THE SURFACE Protect the surface with two coats of acrylic varnish, using matt for a flat finish and satin for more sheen.

Sgraffito

This is a technique traditionally used on ceramics and decorative friezes. It is done by layering two coats of different colours and then scratching through the topcoat to reveal the colour underneath.

Tools & materials

Matt emulsion basecoat
Embossing paste
Trowel
Emulsion brush
Scratching tool such as a pencil with a rubber at the end or a piece of card
Scraper

BASECOAT Paint the wall with the matt emulsion and leave to dry.

APPLYING EMBOSSING PASTE Use the trowel to smooth the embossing paste onto the wall in an arc-shaped motion. Don't worry too much about getting a perfectly smooth finish as a few irregularities add to the look. Allow the paste to firm a little before working on the design. (Follow the manufacturer's guidelines for this, or gently prod with your finger, but do not allow the embossing paste to set too much or you will not be able to draw a design into it.)

MARKING OUT THE DESIGN Experiment by scratching the design onto a piece of card. Bold, graphic designs seem to work best. Using the rubber end of a pencil, a piece of card or even a plastic spatula, scratch the design into the embossing paste. Your scraper should remove the paste to reveal the base colour and create a relief pattern.

VARIATION Embossing paste is usually white, but it can be coloured by adding powder pigment or even fabric dye. Use only a little at a time, as they are very strong.

Rust Effect

Imitating the look of rusting metal may seem strange at first, but it can look fantastic in isolated areas, such as individual panels, offset by pale neutral colours such as pale grey or creamy white. Use sparingly for best effect, as entire walls would be too overpowering. There are two methods: one uses reactive iron paint and the other is a paint effect created using glazes.

Damask

This effect combines several techniques and, like the Moiré Silk Effect (p39), was developed to imitate walls lined with velvet. Choose rambling rose and foliage patterns or make your own stencils based on a fabric you have in your house. Subtle colour shades of white or blue are very effective.

Tools & materials

- Cream matt emulsion basecoat
- Acrylic glaze that can be mixed with emulsion
- White matt emulsion paint
- Darker cream matt emulsion
- Containers for mixing glazes
- Emulsion brushes
- Stippling brush
- Acetate stencil
- Masking tape
- Kitchen paper or rag

BASECOAT Paint the wall with the coloured matt emulsion basecoat. If you want to create more depth in the design you could rag the base colour (see Rag-Rolling p26).

MIXING GLAZE Mix equal parts of the acrylic glaze and the matt white emulsion.

STENCILLING FIRST COAT Attach the acetate stencil to the wall using masking tape. Dip the stippling brush into the glaze, blot off on a piece of kitchen paper or rag and stipple the entire stencil (see Stippling p28). Remove the stencil and repeat the process until the entire area is covered. Leave to dry.

STENCILLING SECOND COAT Mix equal parts of the darker cream matt emulsion and the acrylic glaze. Reposition the stencil and randomly stipple the design again with the darker colour. You are not aiming for complete coverage with the second colour; it is important that some of the white still shows through to create a sense of texture. Repeat until the entire area has been covered and leave to dry.

Tools & materials

Reactive paint method

- Black or very dark brown matt emulsion
- Rust-reactive iron paint
- Ageing solution spray
- Matt acrylic varnish and brush
- Emulsion brushes

Paint-effect method

- Black anti-rust metal gloss paint
- Acrylic glaze
- Raw sienna, dark brown and rusty-red artist's acrylic colour
- Containers for mixing glazes
- Gloss brush
- Sponge
- Water spritzer
- Fitch (optional)
- Satin or matt acrylic varnish and brush

Reactive paint method

INITIAL COATS Paint the surface with the black or dark brown matt emulsion and leave to dry. Then apply a thick, even coat of the rust-reactive iron paint and leave to dry completely.

RUSTING TECHNIQUE Rust the paint by spraying it with the ageing spray; the effect is created as the spray dries. Finish with a coat of matt or satin acrylic varnish.

Paint-effect method

BASECOAT Paint the wall with the black anti-rust metal gloss paint.

MIXING GLAZES Mix three separate glazes with each of the paints. Add paint to the glaze little by little, checking the colour on a piece of scrap paper until the desired density is achieved.

SPONGING COLOUR Starting with the raw sienna glaze, sponge the colour onto the wall (see Sponging p28). Next, sponge on a layer of brown and then a layer of rusty-red glaze. The colours should blend softly into one another, but a little of each coat needs to show through.

ADDING DETAIL To create authentic rust patches, spray water onto the surface and mop it gently with the sponge. You can also stipple colour onto the wall using a fitch. Combine both techniques to create varied texture.

FINISHING Finish with a protective coat of acrylic varnish.

Metallic Effects

Metallic-coloured paints come in a wide range of colours, from natural metallics to rainbow colours. They can be a little tricky to apply, so are best painted on using a roller to prevent brushmarks from showing. Bronzing powders are also available in a wide colour range, including gold, silver, bronze and copper and can be easily mixed with oil- or water-based varnish to create your own paint.

Tools & materials

- Coloured matt emulsion basecoat, close in colour to the metallic powder
- Bronze powder
- Clear satin acrylic varnish
- Container for mixing varnish
- Emulsion brush
- Foam roller and tray
- Varnish brush (optional)

BASECOAT Paint the wall with the coloured matt emulsion and leave it to dry.

MAKING THE VARNISH Next, mix together the varnish and bronzing powder. For every 100ml (4fl oz) acrylic varnish you will need 1 tbsp bronze powder. Stir well.

APPLYING THE VARNISH Use the roller to paint the metallic varnish over the basecoat. It is practically impossible to get a flat, smooth finish with metallic paint; the uneven cover is part of its charm.

PROTECTING Paint a coat of clear acrylic varnish on top of the metallic paint if you want to make it more durable.

Glitter Paints

Ready-mixed glitter 'paints' (essentially a clear varnish in which the glitter is suspended) are available from specialist paint suppliers. Glitter paints need to be painted over a coloured basecoat and the darker the basecoat the more obvious the glitter will be. Glitter paints could also be used over a soft pearlescent basecoat for a shimmering and sparkling effect. Because these paints are quite expensive and fairly limited in the range of colours available, try making your own as described below.

Tools & materials

- Coloured matt emulsion basecoat
- Clear matt acrylic varnish
- Glitter
- Container for mixing varnish and glitter
- Emulsion brush
- Varnish brush

BASECOAT Cover the wall with an even coat of coloured matt emulsion and allow to dry completely.

MIXING VARNISH You cannot store this mixture as the colour from the glitter will bleed into the varnish and tint it, so only mix as much varnish as you can use in one session. For every litre (2 pints) varnish you will need to add roughly 6 tbsp glitter. Stir well.

APPLYING GLITTER VARNISH Paint the glitter varnish onto the wall in even strokes, avoiding overspreading. Stir the varnish and glitter mix often (preferably each time you dip the brush in) so that the particles don't sink to the bottom.

Textured Paint

Although there are a lot of ready-mixed textured paints available, making your own allows you to control the degree of texture and the effect. You can use a variety of materials to add texture including sawdust, sand or even whiting. To work out how much texturizer to add, experiment with a small amount of paint (500ml/1 pint) until you have obtained the effect you require. Then scale up the quantities for a larger area.

Tools & materials

Matt emulsion basecoat
Texturizer such as fine sand, coarse sand, sawdust, or whiting
Coloured matt emulsion
Containers for mixing paint
Acrylic glaze (optional)
Emulsion brushes
Matt acrylic varnish and brush

BASECOAT Pour the correct proportion of basecoat emulsion and your choice of texturizer into a container and mix well. Paint onto the wall and leave to dry.

SECOND COAT You can either paint over the textured basecoat with matt emulsion in the colour of your choice, which will give you a fairly flat finish, or you can use an acrylic glaze coloured with matt emulsion. Using an acrylic glaze applied in loose strokes will allow some of the basecoat to shine through and will create more depth.

VARNISHING Finish the surface with a coat of matt acrylic varnish for a durable finish.

Stamping

This is a simple technique and one that can be used to create interesting details or to cover an entire wall with a single repeating motif. Choose from the large range of ready-made designs available or try making your own from a sponge or a potato.

Tools & materials

Coloured matt emulsion
Small sponge roller and tray
Rubber stamp

COATING THE STAMP Pour the paint into the paint tray and coat the roller in paint. Then use the roller to apply an even layer of paint to the stamp.

APPLYING THE MOTIF Push the stamp onto the wall, rolling it backward and forward, and then remove. Leave to dry.

Experiment with different backgrounds and stamping paints, such as textured grounds and metallic paints. There are a number of specialist shops that can make stamps to your own designs.

pattern

Decorating with pattern is no longer simply a question of papering four matching walls. Used boldly and imaginatively, pattern can combine to create the most dazzling of modern interiors. With this in mind, set aside the rule book and look beyond familiar traditional methods. The new wave of site-specific wallpapers, where a single image made to your dimensions fills an entire wall, is just one approach, elevating wallpaper from a simple backdrop to a work of art.

▲ This Oriental-inspired wallpaper has a diagonal branching pattern and creates a delicate feminine feel in this airy living space.

► The bold diamond pattern of this wallpaper is softened by foliate motifs in the centres. The blue-and-white colour scheme is a classic Scandinavian combination that creates a calm atmosphere.

▼ This drop repeat pattern has a deep purple background and organic metallic motifs that create a series of repeating soft-edged triangles. This creates a modern style with subtle ethnic influences.

With the wide range of designs on offer, it can be difficult to know where to begin, but pattern can be split into two categories, natural and graphic. If you want to include a patterned decorative element in your room, think about the kind of design you prefer. It may be something abstract like a single repeating motif or the bold, super-graphic patterns of the 1970s, or it may be something more naturalistic and less ordered, such as trailing vines and floral motifs.

The style and architecture of your house can be used as a starting point for choosing the way that you use pattern, but avoid trying to slavishly recreate any period look. Instead, take what you like from the era and blend it within a more modern environment to suit the way we live now. If the architecture of your house has a Shaker influence, consider using a traditional hearts-and-flower stencil to decorate the walls in a bedroom, but use a pearlescent paint to give it a modern and subtle twist. Alternatively, use a Shaker colour scheme to paint walls with a bold and graphic border. Decorate walls in a Georgian period home with a pale moiré paint effect to recreate the look of silk-lined walls or alternatively use a damask stencil, painting cream on white for a subtle hint of pattern, introducing a look that is classic as well as modern. Taking such an approach to decorating with pattern means that you are able to work sensitively around the building's character and history without allowing its style to dictate your own.

Using pattern successfully is all about scale and balance. If you love the texture and richness of velvet, for example, but want to retain a feeling of light and air, then using a decorative flock paper on just one wall will add a luxurious element without completely dominating the space. Pull the look together with rich velvet cushions and curtains in complementary tones. Borders and friezes are another option for adding pattern without overpowering the space. Using an unusual placement or proportion, such as an extra-deep border that fills a large section of a wall, will have a more modern feel than a narrow border positioned at traditional dado-height. Don't be afraid to experiment with unusual combinations. Mix large-scale florals with small, single-motif prints, or blend a woodland scene photomural with textured papers and cork. Using a unified colour scheme will ensure that it all combines harmoniously.

photo and single-image walls

Photomurals have been around for some time and could be said to have had their beginnings in the *trompe l'oeil* panels that were popular in France in the 1800s. Although taste in imagery has moved on from the realistic painted swags and pleats of the nineteenth century and we now favour super-real panoramic scenes, the transforming effect of the mural is as dramatic today as it ever was.

Photomurals are essentially the same as the advertising posters plastered over hoardings. They come rolled up in sections and are applied to the wall with paste. Use them in a room that needs a view of its own. If you have an enormous wall that you would like to decorate cheaply, then use a photomural to create a stunning visual effect.

Scenic photomurals were at their height of popularity in the 1960s and 1970s, when they were used to adorn the walls of foyers, dining halls and even bedrooms in hotels. They still bring to mind ski lodges and other now badly dated interiors the world over and their recent revival is due to their kitsch, retro appeal and the trend for making a bold statement. If this is the look for you, create your own scenery with the relaxing view of a palm-fringed, sun-drenched beach; an alpine scene with snow-capped mountains and meadows in flower; or a night-time city skyline with lights twinkling.

You don't necessarily need a massive space to use a photomural: most images can be trimmed to fit your wall without destroying the composition. Don't be deterred from using a photomural even in the smallest room of the house, but keep furnishings simple, to avoid visual over-stimulation.

In recent years there has been a boom in single-image papers, really an extension of the photo mural idea, and providing an easy, modern way to add colour and pattern to a room. Single-image paper can be confined to specific sections of the interior to decorate a dull corner, or can be hung on a main wall in place of all other decoration. The techniques used to create these papers are as varied as the images themselves, and might involve

▸ You can almost smell the damp moss and ferns in this photo wall with an image of an early morning woodland. Applied to the wall and the back of the door so that the door is disguised when closed, this image gives the room a view and a sense of depth.

▸ (overleaf) This large-scale wallpaper of an orchid, designed by Jane Gordon Clark, can be created individually by her company Ornamenta to fill any size wall. It creates an almost surreal effect in the living space; the sheer drama of the image means that no other form of decoration is needed.

digital photography or bespoke hand-printing, which means that you are never confined to a single look.

Digital technology provides endless possibilities in this field. Designer Kate Osborn creates stunning modern murals by enlarging close-up shots of flowers and petals to an enormous scale. Applied to a wall, they take on an abstract quality; the sight of something normally so small reproduced on such a vast scale guarantees a double take. The simplest solution for this type of image is to hang it in the middle of a bare white wall, but it is also possible to wrap it around a corner or over a curved wall or position it off-centre so that it hovers majestically over a sideboard or above a chair.

Create a mural by taking your own pictures, choosing colours that complement your room scheme. Natural images work well: close-ups of flowers, moss on a wall or a shot of shadows on water can result in amazing abstract patterns. For a more urban feel you might consider shop signs, streetlights, or architectural features such as railings and brickwork. The image can then be enlarged digitally at a photographic shop and pasted on the wall. (For more ideas see the project on p54.)

The work of Tracy Kendall features delicate prints inspired by nature, including feathers, seed heads and skeletal foliage, which are refined to their purest elements and magnified so that each image stretches over a couple of metres. Printed in a single colour, the effect is still and calming. Some prints are further adorned with sequins, loose threads, crystals and beads, adding a light-catching three-dimensional quality. These papers have the most impact when they are hung as panels.

Decorating a wall in this way means that you will need to think carefully about the placement of the other elements in the room. Placing furniture in front of or against a large-scale graphic image can interfere with the effect and chop the design in half visually, so experiment with the layout of your room and how the elements will balance before fixing the banners to the wall.

▲ Try pasting a large-scale map onto your walls as an alternative to wallpaper; sea charts or musical manuscripts can also work well.

▶ A palm-fringed beach mural and animal-print sofa combine to create a tropical, fun-filled atmosphere in this living room.

LUXOR
Vegas
THE MIRAGE
CAESARS PALACE

Blown-Up Image

This is an effective way of creating a focal point in the bedroom or on any wall that needs a lift. Think carefully about what images you want to use. A series of sea images patchworked together will create a calming modern photomural and a textural detail of lichen or a shot of peeling paint would be suitable for an abstract panel. Landscape-format pictures work well above a bed if they are butted up together and used two or three pictures deep. Square pictures allow you to play more with the positioning. Try turning some on their sides or upside down, so that familiar images become more abstract.

Tools & materials

ENLARGED PHOTOGRAPHS
POLYBOARD
PHOTOMOUNT ADHESIVE SPRAY
CRAFT KNIFE
STEEL RULER
SELF-ADHESIVE HOOK-AND-LOOP VELCRO TAPE
SPIRIT LEVEL

Method

1. A photographic lab will enlarge your images to the size required. It is possible to get pictures enlarged up to A0 size (91.5 x 127cm/36 x 50in).
2. Mount the images onto the polyboard using the photomount adhesive spray. Take care to mask off surrounding areas and follow the manufacturer's directions.
If necessary, trim the image and board with a craft knife and steel ruler.
3. Stick self-adhesive hook-and-loop Velcro tape to the back of each image and attach to the wall (see below centre). When sticking the images onto the wall, start in the centre and work outwards, using the spirit level to make sure that they are perfectly straight (see below left).
4. If you are using the same image for the entire panel, think about positioning some upside down. If your images are in a square format, then quarter-turn some of them to create visual interest.

repetition

The inventive repetition of single images can create patterns in quite different ways. Using a single motif or even several motifs that repeat in sequence to decorate walls has the potential to create a bold and striking effect. Take the simplest pattern of all, the dot; teeny-weeny polka dots can have a very soft effect when used in pale shades giving walls a slightly textured look and creating a rhythmic pattern. However, if the dot is blown up so that its diameter measures over 50cm (20in) and used in a rigid grid pattern, then the look takes on a graphic form and makes an uncompromisingly modern statement.

Any geometric shape – from rectangles to rhomboids – can be used to create a simple pattern. It can be helpful to use colour to define a mood and to build movement into the pattern that you are creating. Using monochrome combinations such as black and white, red and white or grey and white to depict a large repeated image would make a striking impact. The same image used with a range of three tonally similar colours will have a calming effect but could start to look too dull, so experiment by using one denser, more saturated shade. If you don't want the darker shade to overpower your pattern, use it in equal amounts to the two other softer shades, distributing it evenly throughout. Finally, adopt and be inspired by the colours that you have chosen in your furnishing fabrics and accessories for a harmonious scheme.

Pattern does not have to be used all over a wall: indeed when used in the form of a border or frieze it can help to shift the visual focus in a room. Initially based on Greek and Roman patterns, friezes have always responded to the visual style of the day, reflecting, for example, the popularity of chinoiserie in the eighteenth century, or the Gothic revival of the Victorian age. In the eighteenth century onwards, interiors with plaster walls were topped with ornately moulded plaster friezes that were hand-painted and often gilded, while Arts and Crafts and Art Nouveau homes combined

▲ Large black circles make a bold visual statement in this monochromatic living room.

▶ Slabs of subtle colour make a basic checked pattern in this hallway. By using darker shades at the bottom of the wall and lighter shades at the top, the onlooker's eye is naturally encouraged to follow the line of the industrial staircase. This effect can be created by painting colours around the wall in a rectangular grid.

to think
clearly
you need
shadows

stencilling along with machine- and hand-painted borders to add definition at ceiling height. All these devices employ the use of repetitive patterns and provide many ideas – both for flat surface patterns and for more three-dimensional forms – that can be adapted today.

A simple border running above doorways and just below the ceiling will draw the eye upwards and help to increase the sense of height in the room. Avoid using colours that are dark and instead paint your ceiling a receding colour such as white or pale blue. Using a warm, advancing colour such as red will have the opposite effect and make the ceiling feel lower.

Avoid restricting your approach to pattern by simply looking at wallpaper or stencilled borders. Think of the basic colours and shapes of children's games to give imagery for decorating the walls in a baby's or teenager's bedroom. For a more traditional approach, scour auctions for old print books of birds, flowers and fauna and use them to

▲ A Greek key motif painted around the top of the room draws the eye up and gives a dynamic contrast with the strong yellow walls. The overall effect of the colour scheme is fresh and vibrant.

► Old botanical prints have been used as an imaginative alternative to wallpaper and, in combination with the cracking plaster below it, give this room a gently aged look.

◄ Here the wall has been divided into a grid and motifs placed in each rectangle. This is a good way of spacing pattern to give a structure to the various elements of a design. Tones of yellow, orange and cream give the room a bright and energetic feel.

create sequences of repeated images that resemble wallpaper. The pages can be left untouched or, alternatively, can be softly tinted with inks. If you decide to colour the pages and if the paper is thin, you may need to stretch it: this means that when you paste it onto the walls it will dry flat and will not wrinkle. Andy Warhol-style prints would also work well used in this way to create a more colourful, bold look that sits well with retro furniture and modern elements.

When covering a wall with old prints, consider carefully where and how you position them. Covering one wall provides an interesting talking point, whereas covering an entire room can change the impression from a room with a lively element to one with a distracting, claustrophobic interior. When you are using repeated images you should also consider how the wall decoration of one room flows into the next living space, particularly important with a bold or eccentric design. If the wall you have covered with large rectangles or prints has a doorway opening on to an adjacent room then strengthen the statement and link the two by repeating the image on a different scale or on a different surface in the next room. Having complementary colour schemes within adjoining rooms will help achieve this.

Repeated images can also be used to improve awkward spaces. A narrow hall that has a painted image of a cresting wave in the style of a Japanese print will give it a dynamic rhythm that creates energy and movement down the length of the hall. Similarly, an elegant script that flows around the top of a wall just below the ceiling can serve to make a large-proportioned room feel more intimate. This technique also suits the familiar, comforting style of certain kitchens where the names of herbs can be painted or stencilled above white bevelled tiles. Enscribed in a rich chocolate brown colour, this is a chic touch that can successfully draw together the various elements of the room.

▸ This wallpaper featuring monochromatic prints of horses creates an authentic country air in the room. The same design in fabric used as a tablecloth in the dining room helps to link the two rooms.

stencilling & stamping

After their popularity in the 1980s, stencilling and stamping have fallen out of favour in recent years and as a result have become rather under-used techniques. However, as with many age-old methods, new generations will always find ways of reinventing them to suit their contemporary tastes. So set aside any thoughts of using country-style motifs reminiscent of the 1980s, because there are now numerous examples of pre-cut designs on the market that reflect the fashions of the day. Large-scale roses stencilled in a grid pattern in strong pinks have a 1950s retro appeal that is also right up to date, while polka dots or stencils of elegant shoes with pointed toes and kitten heels will add an element of fun to a bedroom or dressing area.

Stencilling (see p29 for technique) doesn't have to be limited to the traditional repeating border, as there is a very wide choice of large-scale panel designs available. Try stencilling a giant fern leaf at a height of 1.5m (5ft) along the wall of a hallway and up the stairs. A large-scale Buddha figure will work well stencilled using rich, spice colours, and stylized floral motifs in black or grey over a strong red background will give a room a definitive Eastern slant. Often the simplest designs are the best: for a dizzying optical effect use two dot stencils in different sizes and randomly overlap them.

Stamping (see p43 for technique) is a technique that is even simpler and quicker than stencilling. It simply involves rolling paint onto the stamp and pressing it onto the wall. It is possible to make your own stamps out of practically any material, from potatoes to sponges or fine-foam rubber, or you can choose to buy them ready made. If you are making your own stamps, then choose simple shapes such as geometric patterns or folk-art inspired designs, as they will be much easier to cut. Another idea is to look through old embroidery catalogues for motifs that will be easy to copy.

▸ The combination of an ogee-shaped headboard and cherry-blossom stencils give this bedroom theme a distinctly Oriental air.

▾ Overlapping polka dots create a blurred effect on the walls that softens the monochromatic colour scheme in this living room. Attention is drawn to the fireplace wall with repeating black-on-white flower stencils.

Gloss Stencil

A new approach to stencilling that moves definitively away from the peachy-coloured trailing vines of past stencilling styles, this project uses brilliant colour and pattern. Rather than picking out a traditional damask pattern in realistic shades, both the matt base and the gloss stencil use the same bold, shocking pink, and introduce subtle patterned elements to the walls. Where you are in the room and the quality of the light will determine how much of the pattern is visible. Position the border just below the ceiling or above the skirting board (base board) and avoid running it around the middle of the wall as this will cut the room in half.

Tools & materials

SHOCKING PINK MATT EMULSION

SHOCKING PINK GLOSS PAINT

ACETATE STENCIL

SPIRIT LEVEL

LOW-TACK MASKING TAPE

PENCIL

EMULSION BRUSH

LARGE STIPPLING BRUSH

PAINT TRAY FOR GLOSS PAINT

Method

1. Paint the wall with an even basecoat of matt emulsion and allow to dry completely.
2. Position the stencil on the wall, using a spirit level to make sure that it is straight, and secure with the masking tape. Use low-tack masking tape, or blot ordinary masking tape onto a piece of fabric to reduce its stickiness and prevent it from peeling the paint off the wall. Mark the stencil's position with a pencil.
3. Position the stencil to create a repeating pattern along the wall, marking with a pencil where each stencil starts and finishes. When you start to stencil you will use these as guidelines, so you can work on every other stencil without overlapping onto any wet paint and smudging your design.
4. Pour a small amount of gloss paint into the tray. Using the large stipple brush, dab it in the gloss and onto a piece of card to avoid overloading the brush with paint. Then dab the brush through the stencil to pick out the pattern.
5. Carefully remove the stencil and move it to the next-but-one position, matching it to the marks you made earlier. Stipple as before and repeat until the pattern is complete.

For more information on stippling and stencilling techniques see pp28–29.

◂ (step 2) Position the stencil on the wall using a spirit level to make sure that it is straight. Fix it either with low-tack masking tape or repositionable adhesive spray.

▶ (step 4) Dab the stipple brush in the gloss paint and onto a piece of card to avoid overloading the brush. Then dab the brush through the stencil to pick out the pattern.

▸ Gloss paint in the same colour as the emulsion paint has been used to pick out the pattern of the stencil on the wall. Experiment with a pearlescent paint over a similar colour of base paint to create a more shimmering effect.

combining pattern

In a feature for the magazine *Nest* in Spring 2002, Joseph Holtzman writes about the rudiments of good wallpaper design and explains that: 'The pattern should work as a frame for things you hang over it and should not overpower them. At the same time the wallpaper and its repeats should register when it has been largely covered over, from whatever remains visible.' This advice is useful when you are decorating a whole room with pattern. It is important to vary the scale, from large, bold prints to small sprigs or tiny checks. Using prints of the same scale all over the room would be both dull and overpowering. Likewise, too many patterns jumbled together can be equally distracting; with no focal point, the eye will recoil in confusion. To balance the effect, select patterns that match your chosen colour scheme. If you were planning to use a large, thick stripe on the walls then use a narrow stripe on the furnishings in the same colour range. Blend in some plain panels of colour and the occasional plain surface, such as a wall, to provide some respite from the patterns. You will find that some areas of calm will actually enhance the effect.

Pattern plays a vital part in creating optical illusions (a camouflage print is the most obvious example), and can be used to enhance your room's best features while at the same time downplaying its weaknesses. Stripes are an excellent tool for increasing the sense of space in a room: when used horizontally they will widen a wall and if used vertically they will add height. If you would like to draw attention away from a dark and dull corner, then position a bold, large-scale print on an opposite wall. A rich floral design will help to disguise uneven walls, as the movement of the pattern will distract the eye from the wall's imperfections.

Patterns are not only about disguise, but can also be used for definition. Patterns designed along a branching diagonal line are excellent for halls and stairs as they guide the eye along and upwards.

▸ This floral wallpaper is reminiscent of Jacobean crewelwork, but, used on just one wall and combined with a bold floral rug and modern furniture it has a confident, modern style.

▾ Gingham goes large scale in this dining room: used all over the walls, and on the table, it creates a fresh and homely environment.

Different sized prints can be used effectively to define different areas of a room. For example, a large floral print can be used to identify the sleeping zone and a matching, smaller-scale floral print can be used to define the dressing area.

If you are using one pattern to cover all your walls, then choose something that is reasonably non-directional and non-representational, such as a paisley or an abstract floral. In this way the pattern will not overpower the space but will act as a backdrop that can be seen in certain places, perhaps where it is juxtaposed with a piece of furniture or where it draws attention to the shape of a vase placed against it. When you are choosing pattern for a room, take into account the patterns already in situ, such as the grain of wooden floors and furniture, or the design of artwork, carpets and architectural details. The room may have an inherent geometric pattern, such as the herringbone design of parquet flooring, or the repeat pattern of egg-and-dart plaster moulding. Such a combination of patterns will create a different visual effect than, for example, more flowing organic designs, and provides a starting point that the wall treatment can sensitively complement to ensure the room works as a whole.

To get an idea of how a combination of patterns will work, collect swatches of each design and pin them next to each other. This will help you to identify what elements leap out. If the wallpaper is the strongest feature, is it a successful juxtaposition with other elements or is it too powerful? You might decide to choose a less dominant pattern or restrict it to one or two walls only. Paint the remaining walls a co-ordinating but calming colour, such as soft blue, beige or light green, all restful colours on the eye. Look carefully at the motifs you have chosen. You can mix two large-scale patterns if the imagery is related; if not, opt for a second pattern with a smaller scale.

▲ This room uses pattern successfully by using one unifying colour scheme and combining different scales of chintzy floral patterns on both walls and furnishings.

▶ (overleaf) Inspired by classical architecture, the wallpaper in the reception room of the Villa di Geggianno in Italy adds structure to the walls and sits well with the curving lines and the hand-painted motifs on the furniture.

wallpaper

The term 'wallpaper' covers a multitude of options, from the tacky glitz of gold gravel stuck onto paper to the low-key floral repeats of a country-style room. One recent innovation involves lengths of orange rubber fastened only at the top and bottom of a wall, which can then be pulled out and used to stash books, piles of clothes and even bedlinen. Ordinary printed papers seem mundane by comparison, but even here the range of designs is bewildering.

The evolution of wallpaper was dictated by developments in paper production, which first began in China in the second century. In Europe, it wasn't until the fifteenth century that paper was made in large enough quantities to be used for anything other than books. The first wallpapers came to Europe from China and were hand-painted lengths depicting tropical birds and flowers or scenes from everyday Chinese life. Each length was unique and incredibly expensive, and was therefore bought only by the wealthy. These Chinese papers led to a trend for Oriental-styled rooms, which were furnished with lacquered cabinets, silks and blue and white ceramics. Many European country houses still have a chinoiserie room, often with the original paper intact.

Around the 1750s the development of block printing meant that wallpaper was more readily available, although the results were variable. Flock was particularly popular and was even used by Madame de Pompadour, mistress of Louis XV and patron of arts and literature, to decorate rooms at Versailles. While the eighteenth-century fashion was for elegant floral decoration, the mass markets and mechanization of the nineteenth century led to a change in tastes and design. Natural imagery was still popular, especially super-realistic floral designs, but these were overtaken by a desire for *trompe l'oeil* papers that reproduced the effects of ruched silk or muslin. Imitation plaster and cornicing was also hugely popular, especially in a grisaillé colourway that mimicked the colours of the originals.

The distinctive designs of William Morris had a huge influence on wallpaper. He advocated using nature as inspiration without copying it slavishly, and created structured patterns, usually in a diagonal branch form, a diamond-shaped net or a simple grid. This meant that his work was both natural and geometric. Art Nouveau grew out of Morris's Arts and Crafts movement and adopted the same naturalistic influences but exaggerated the form to create very different results.

Art Deco designs dominated the interwar years and wallpaper became much more graphic. Inspired by Cubist paintings and jazz, patterns were bold and geometric. Wallpaper borders were also used extensively below the picture rail or above the dado and were in striking contrast to the wallpaper, which often featured black backgrounds with strong, interwoven designs in bright colours.

The 1950s and 1960s saw the development of modernism, and large-scale abstract pattern became a standard. There were also considerable technological developments at this time, as pre-trimmed and ready-pasted papers came onto the market, along with washable vinyl designs.

There are now so many types of design that almost anything goes, but it is our application of wallpaper that has changed. Instead of covering all four walls, we can invest in a more expensive paper to create a single, feature wall. Modern furniture might be casually teamed with old-fashioned chintzy florals for an eclectic mix, while traditional Anaglypta, no longer confined to the area below the dado rail, might be painted in daring, modern shades of black or gold over an entire wall. Fashion trends are translated into wallpapers more rapidly than ever before. And although the trend for *trompe l'oeil* papers hasn't gone away, it is no longer for realistic country scenes or architectural details but for tread-plate metal, brick, wood grain, gravel or even the sky. This is all part of a style in which the mundane and everyday are reinvented by a change of colour, scale and application.

◂ Matt printed colour and metallic foil create a textural, striated pattern that works with the 1960s' furniture without dominating the room or making it feel darker.

▸ The graphic circles design wallpaper by Ulf Moritz gives this study a dark, cosy atmosphere.

▾ (above) Elegantly trailing eighteenth-century style wallpaper offsets the modern classic 'Butterfly' stool designed by Sori Yanagi in 1956.

▾ (below) This less conventional use of wallpaper applies a single strip in a horizontal direction, offsetting the plain colour of the wall behind.

▲ Monochromatic colour schemes can be harsh: a stylized, close-repeat flower print wallpaper helps to create a more relaxed feel without deviating from the black-and-white theme.

▶ The sophisticated combination of a pale grey/lilac ground and a delicate damask pattern demonstrates the modern reinvention of flocked wallpaper. However it is co-ordinated, it will ensure a sumptuous setting.

Floral-Border Wallpaper

A new, and hopefully more tasteful, take on the ultra popular, narrow wallpaper borders of the late 1980s. Rather than simply applying a width of wallpaper horizontally around the room, sections of the background are cut away. This makes the edges less defined and allows the pattern to merge with the wall. Floral or trellis wallpapers work particularly well because the pattern tends to flow continually without breaking up, leaving you with one piece of lacy paper rather than lots of bits of pattern that have separated as you cut away the ground.

Obviously the more intricate the pattern the longer it will take to cut out, so if you wish to cover a large area with the wallpaper border then choose a simple pattern unless you have plenty of time and lots of patience. This device works well used along the walls of an empty hallway or passage adding interest and decorative detail.

Tools & materials

PATTERNED WALLPAPER

CRAFT KNIFE

CUTTING MAT

WALLPAPER PASTE AND BRUSH

SPIRIT LEVEL

CHALK

DAMP CLOTH

Method

1. Using a craft knife and cutting mat, cut away sections of the background from your wallpaper to the length required (see below left). Turn the paper over and gently brush on the wallpaper paste, allowing it to sink in for five minutes.
2. Using a spirit level, chalk a bottom line onto your wall against which you can hang the wallpaper. Line the wallpaper up with the bottom line and smooth the paper onto the wall in an upwards and outwards motion (see below right). Make sure there is no air trapped and that the paper is hung straight. Wipe away any excess paste with a damp cloth.

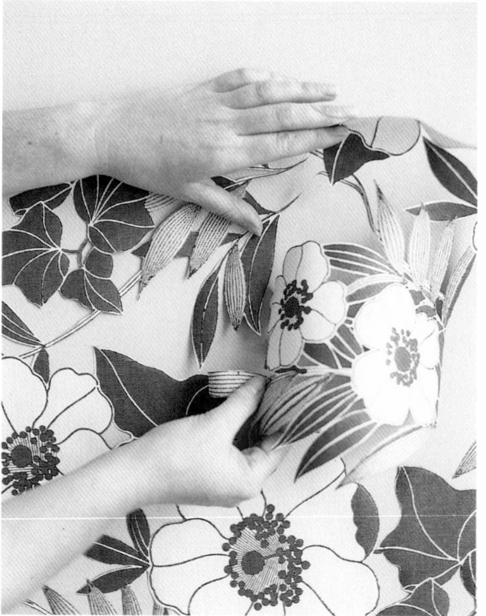

texture

A home should stimulate all your senses, including touch. Introducing a tactile element to walls will help to enhance the atmosphere of a room, whether you are after the coolness of rough, limewashed plaster, or the rich pattern and warmth of natural cork. Textural elements not only enhance a room's visual dynamics, but also appeal to our instinctive enjoyment of different materials.

▲ Chipboard tends to be a behind-the-scenes material, yet it clads the walls of this bedroom creating a warm, lived-in feel.

► Bare brick painted in a rich chocolate brown gives this wall a sophisticated facelift without detracting from its rustic appeal. It also provides the perfect foil for the heavily grained, retro wooden furniture. Experiment with eggshell paint, which has a soft, sheeny finish, or alternatively gloss, which will reflect more light and have a cooler feel.

Think about contrasting textural experiences by placing the rough with the smooth. In a modern, urban setting, low-tech materials such as fibreboard sheets add warmth and intimacy and will enhance the smooth, gentle sheen of materials such as polished concrete or plaster.

Textured wallcoverings can be used to create a sense of luxury – after all, what could be more decadent than walls clad with leather or suede? Because of the expense, these materials are often confined to smaller rooms such as the study, conjuring up images of secret, smoky gentleman's clubs lit by soft pools of light. At the other extreme – and much less subtle – flock, invented as a cheaper alternative to the Italian silks popular in the eighteenth century, blends texture with pattern and colour. Although flock has a certain kitsch appeal today, it makes an undeniably dramatic statement.

The feature wall has become a popular decorating device and often includes a retro-revival theme. Stone cladding, not so long ago deemed deeply tasteless, has made a comeback, along with pine, cork tiles and textured geometric papers. These materials provide an element of warmth and cosy familiarity, yet are strikingly contemporary when combined with starker modern designs.

The trend for a modern rustic style has also increased the popularity of textured walls. Exposed brick is left untouched, rough plaster is lightly washed with a pale tint and a new breed of textured paints has appeared. More advanced than the earlier sand-and-sawdust textured paints, these are designed to create the effect of cord or even suede when brushed onto walls.

There has also been a revival in the use of traditional plaster finishes. Pitted plaster, which has the appearance of honed or lightly polished limestone, has been popularized by its use in chic fashion stores and hotels. The burred and marbled effect of marmorino stucco, used extensively during the Renaissance period as a background for frescoes, is cool to the touch due to the amount of moisture it retains, and creates an almost temple-like atmosphere of calm when used in the home.

Textured walls are somehow easier on the eye and to the touch than dead-flat painted surfaces. They also add depth to a room by reflecting and absorbing light. It is perhaps no coincidence that these materials often relate directly to nature: wood, cork, stone and even raffia papers bring the outside indoors, and comfort and soothe our senses with their elemental textures.

To get a sense of just how important texture is, consider how we are affected by unappealing sensations. If we don't like the way something feels against our skin then no matter how attractive its appearance, we cannot live with it.

Inspiration for texture can be found everywhere, so look for visual stimuli when you are thinking about introducing textural elements in the home. Think about what kinds of textures you enjoy: is it the feeling of sand between your toes; the cool, smooth finish of stone; or the warm, rough and uneven texture of bark and cork? Play one type of texture off another by positioning the glassy finish of lacquer and gloss paint alongside the more gritty surface of a wall rendered with gravel.

Many paint techniques, such as wood graining (see p32), are designed to emulate the effect of a textured surface, but some techniques, such as combing (see p27), have a real texture of their own. The latter is traditionally done in small areas but can create a dramatic textured statement. Try using a large comb to drag random, sweeping lines across a wall covered with glaze. Then go back over it to create a network of striated lines. If you apply the glaze quite thickly, but not so thickly that it runs, the effect will be more noticeable. For a similar pattern with more relief try using the sgraffito technique (see p40). Use a neutral beige base with a white overlay to create an interesting backdrop for dark wood furniture and a sisal carpet.

Sponging (see p28) and rag rolling (see p24) are paint effects that will create an illusion of depth and richness. Using rich shades of brown and ochre will evoke aged leather, while pale grey colours will emulate the mottled surface of stone. For something more stone-like without going to the expense of cladding, create your own stone effect (see p34) by painting blocks or bricks onto the walls. Choose colours that resemble natural stone as closely as possible for a *trompe l'oeil* finish.

Crackling or *craquelure* (see p30) creates the beautiful aged effect of peeling wood or varnish

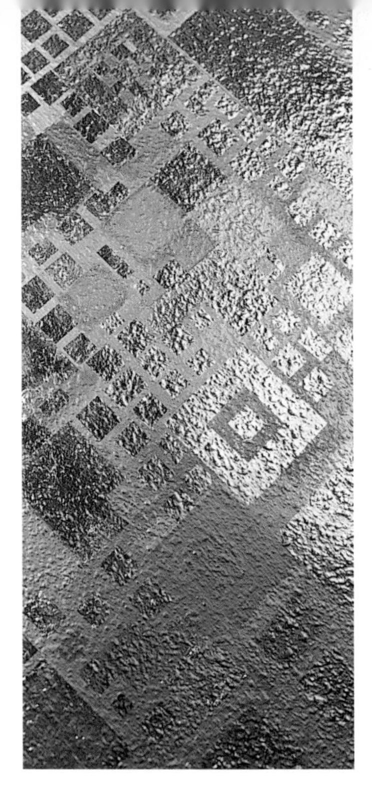

▲ Woodchip wallpaper lends a textural finish to this wall that has been stencilled and gilded with an abstract geometric pattern to create a rich and complex design.

► Washes of colour ranging from light khaki to deep green have been laid over each other in random strokes and rubbed with a cloth to give this wall a sense of depth.

▼ Spatter painting creates a lightly textured pattern and an authentic backdrop to the Italian-style furniture in this Swedish home.

and is a relatively simple technique to achieve. It can be used on practically any surface, from wood to laminate. For a Scandinavian look, choose grey-whites and smoky-blues and use to age mouldings with a gilded or silvered surface.

There is a variety of pre-mixed textured paints on the market. Stone-fleck spray can be used to build up a stone finish, but because of its expense is best used for small areas only. Denim paint has a slightly gritty consistency, and can be used to re-create the look of woven fabric. Apply it using a dragging technique (see p25), first vertically, and then horizontally, to create the effect of weft and warp.

Cord paint is fairly coarse and is designed to be rollered onto the wall and then worked with a stiff brush while still wet to make a corded texture. This effect can be overwhelming in large quantities so is best limited to one or two walls.

It is possible to make textured paint by adding sand or sawdust to a pre-mixed water-based paint

◀ Ultramarine tinted limewash integrates well with the exposed ceiling beams in this country house. For a more subtle effect, try mixing a creamy beige pigment with the limewash mix.

▲ The crackle-glaze effect used in this stark hallway helps to make it feel less austere and complements the chalky green of the Scandinavian clock.

▶ This mottled wall-paint effect draws the room's colour scheme into the heavy shades of rich purples and blues. The unexpected effect of the niche between the fireplace and door and the white wall behind is a dramatic interruption that lifts and enriches the effect of these deep colours.

with either a matt or satin finish. Any type of sand is suitable, and obviously the coarser sands will produce a more textured result. Paint textured in this way has a rustic effect and is good for disguising uneven walls. Try using it over brick or even breeze blocks to enhance the natural texture.

The way that you apply the paint will produce different results. A large, long-bristled brush and loose, random brushstrokes will create a country feel. For a more subtle effect, use fine sand in a soft-coloured basecoat and apply with a fine-bristled brush. Finish with a glaze coat in the same soft colour as the basecoat for a gently textured finish.

▲ This grey-toned exterior wall has a rough, unfinished texture that is the perfect foil to a mass of brightly coloured flowers and lush foliage.

◄ Rough and smooth textures and neutral and bright colours play off each other on adjacent walls in this classic 1990s'-style bedroom.

► A rubbed-back plaster finish lends this living room a relaxed and calm atmosphere that sits comfortably with the natural wood surfaces and informal, time-worn furniture.

bricks & stone

Since the mass development of loft-space living we have come to associate bare brick walls with urban spaces. Uncovered brick walls seem to go naturally with industrial metal-framed windows, iron girders and concrete flooring. Yet this wasn't always the case: in the 1950s and 1960s thin slips of brick were applied to walls, especially around the fireplace, to give rooms warmth and texture. It seems that each generation finds its own way to use brick as part of its interior decoration.

If you have an exposed brick wall that needs cleaning it can be sandblasted or treated with strong chemicals, although this is a messy business. An alternative is to treat stubborn stains with a paste made from fuller's earth or ground chalk mixed with white spirit. Wipe more white spirit over the stain, then spread the paste on top and tape a plastic bag or aluminium foil over it. This will act as a poultice, which you can leave for a couple of days to draw out the stain.

Interior brick walls also look good when painted. Painting allows the textured finish to show through, but gives you more flexibility with the colour scheme. White is a safe option, but brick can look stunning painted a velvety black or deep aubergine colour. Dark chocolate works well with polished concrete or limestone floors and a thin line of mint green paint drawn three-quarters of the way up the wall or about 50cm (20in) from the floor will freshen and lift the colour. Accessorize with mint green vases and vessels to pull the look together.

Thin brick tiles are perfect for cladding and come in all designs and materials. Concrete cladding bricks are a pale grey colour and have various textures. Rather than covering a whole wall, apply a wide band across the centre for a raised textural contrast to plaster. Vertical stripes, circles, or even a herringbone pattern can have an equally strong visual impact because of the contrast between smooth plaster and rough brick. Decorative concrete building blocks also have a place and could be used to build a dividing wall in a living area or kitchen dining-space.

▲ The stone walls in this cottage have been left exposed, providing a focal point and bedhead in this natural-style bedroom.

▸ The white walls in this monochromatic living space allow the pattern of the brickwork to show through, giving extra textural interest to the interior.

▲ The rough surface and warm colours of these bare brick walls are a reminder of the building's industrial heritage. The low-level Eastern-style sofa and the bold light fitting help to draw attention to the exposed brick and the tiled, barrel-vaulted ceiling.

◂ Polished plaster has a smooth, creamy finish with a mottled surface and can also be tinted with a range of tones. Natural plaster shades work well as a backdrop for strong hits of colour such as the red embroidered bedspread used in this bedroom.

▸ Often the simplest methods of decorating are the best. Here uneven, thickly plastered walls are painted brilliant white, juxtaposed with highlights of navy blue and simple furnishings.

plaster

Coloured and polished hard plaster was first used in buildings by the ancient Egyptians. This was later refined by the Greeks, who used it in the palace at Knossos, and by the Romans at Pompeii. The most lavish and decorative use of plaster, in the form of stucco and marmorino, took place during the Renaissance, particularly in Venice and Florence.

Marmorino is an incredibly versatile material and can be tinted to practically any colour. Made from lime, cement, marble dust, pigments and oils, it is applied in fine layers by hand with a trowel. The addition of the marble dust allowed the Italians of the Renaissance to re-create the look of marble cladding at a fraction of the cost and weight. These qualities make marmorino still attractive to us today. Its versatility means it can be used for a number of different effects, from the soft, blurred look of marble and the smooth, glassy finish of stucco lustro, to a pitted finish with the feel of honed or polished limestone. The grainy surface and slate-grey colour of the limestone-effect looks strikingly modern, yet the technique and material are centuries old.

Stucco and marmorino have very pristine finishes and should be carried out by an expert. However, there are a number of plaster finishes that can be done at home and which only need a little practice to create successfully. A polished plaster finish (see p36) is a relatively simple technique, but you do need to be able to plaster a wall and achieve a completely flat finish. An electric polisher will give you the best sheen and, as long as you use a polished plaster mix, the end result will be softly and unevenly coloured. For a really high shine, apply a coat of clear wax and polish with an electric sander; for a softer sheen polish by hand. A faux-plaster effect, similar to the visual style of the walls of Mediterranean houses, can be achieved by rubbing a layer of whiting and pigment into wax. The resulting effect is that of old paint brushed onto ageing plaster. This finish allows you to be adventurous with colour, as bright shades work just

▾ Creamy, rough-plastered walls and smooth polished concrete floors have been used to create a modern rustic look in this living room. The walls are left bare, creating a cool, contemplative atmosphere.

as well as softer, more natural tones, but for the best results work on a white base. (For technique see Mock Plaster p38.) Another faux-plaster finish that can be achieved using paint techniques is the fresco effect (see p38), based on the traditional method of applying colour to wet plaster. The finished look is very similar to the old frescos seen in Italian churches and palaces and it can be used to give new walls or plaster mouldings an aged appearance.

The rubbed-back plaster finish (see p37) is an easy technique for instantly ageing walls and involves painting glazes mixed with whiting onto the wall, and then rubbing back with sandpaper. It uses a similar technique to limewashing and works best using soft, pastel-coloured glazes. Rough plaster and distressed plaster (see pp36 and 37) are two of the more hardcore techniques – they are very effective and dramatic, but you do need to be sure that these are the effects that you really want, because once you start there is no going back!

For a rough plaster finish, trowel plaster onto the wall in a fairly thin layer and then skim over the top with a decorator's float. You can then use colour glazes to build up the effect. Allowing the glaze to settle in the hollows and cracks will help to accentuate the uneven texture of the wall, while finishing with a wash of white will knock the colour back and give it a softly aged feel. Distressed plaster (see p37) will create a finish that looks as if the walls have not been touched for centuries. If you are after the well-worn, crumbling look, with patches of faded colour, then this is definitely the effect to use.

▸ The warm pink tones of a freshly plastered wall have a beautiful decorative quality in their own right. If you choose to leave them untouched, paint woodwork in pristine white for a fresh feel and to establish that this is a carefully considered decorative option.

Raised Plaster Stencil

A textural alternative to flat colour stencilling, this technique works well with either single motifs positioned randomly or with a repeating pattern. While it is tricky to get it absolutely perfect, the imperfections generally add to the rustic charm. Use it on roughly plastered colourwashed walls (see page 24 for colourwashing technique and recipe) or on perfectly plastered walls for a cleaner look. Use gesso rather than ordinary plaster to pick out the pattern, as this is easier to work with, and always use an acetate stencil because it is simpler to clean and much more flexible.

You can buy ready-made gesso that you melt in a bain-marie to a workable consistency or you can make your own, the recipe for which is below. If you buy ready-made gesso you need follow from step 5. If you do decide to make your own gesso it can be stored in the fridge for a couple of days, so only mix what you think you will need.

Tools & materials

30G (1OZ) RABBITSKIN GRANULES
TWO BOWLS, ONE SMALLER THAN THE OTHER, TO MAKE BAIN-MARIE
500ML (17FL OZ) WATER
1KG (2 LB) WHITING
ACETATE STENCIL
MASKING TAPE
PALETTE KNIFE
CLOTHS

Method

1. Put the rabbitskin granules into the smaller bowl and cover with 250ml (8fl oz) of water and leave to soak overnight.
2. Add the rest of the water.
3. Pour very hot (but not boiling) water into the larger bowl and sit the smaller bowl in it. Stir to make sure all the rabbitskin granules have dissolved.
4. As the water cools, replenish with more hot water, as the mixture needs to be kept fairly warm to remain workable.
5. Pour the whiting in bit by bit, stirring all the time to avoid lumps, until the gesso has nearly reached the consistency of double cream.
6. Position your stencil on the wall using the masking tape.
7. Working from the bottom to the top, apply a thin layer of gesso over the stencil using the palette knife. You are aiming for a layer that is about the same thickness as lightweight card.
8. Carefully peel the stencil off trying not to knock the gesso. Clean both sides of the stencil with a damp cloth so it does not clog.

For more information on stencilling techniques see p29.

PURE BRISTLES
STERILIZED
MADE IN ENGLAND

◄ (step 3) The gesso mixture needs to be heated gently in a bain-marie until all the rabbitskin granules have dissolved and the mixture has reached a workable texture.

► (step 7) Using a palette knife, spread a thin layer of gesso over the stencil.

textured papers

The desire to break away from plain flat surfaces and introduce texture on walls has led to a radical new approach to wallpaper. The old staple decorating materials that had completely fallen out of favour, such as paper-backed hessian (burlap), are once again in high demand and have led to the appearance of more sophisticated natural-fibre papers. Raffia has a natural basketweave pattern and comes in a range of both neutral and bright colours, while grasscloth papers range from fine to very textured and are perfect for creating a neutral but tactile backdrop. Natural-fibre papers can be trickier to hang than ordinary papers, but there is the bonus when using these of not having to match a pattern repeat. If hanging grass or reed fibre on your wall is just that little bit too rough-hewn for you, there are plenty of imitation papers that have the same richly textured look and include split-bamboo and wood-grain patterns.

Other textured papers include Anaglypta or low-relief papers. These were developed in the 1870s and were used extensively in hallways below the dado rail in this period because of their durability. They are great for use on walls with less-than-perfect surfaces as their texture will disguise any surface irregularities, and can be painted to co-ordinate with your interior. If this is too reminiscent of woodchip, you may be surprised by the large and varied selection of textured papers to choose from, with designs ranging from brightly coloured raised circles and squares to elegant white low-relief stripes and woven patterns.

Flock has to be the most decadent textured wallpaper of all. Its patterns and textures come from glueing velvet pile in a pattern to a paper backing. It works well in rooms with high ceilings and classical proportions but can also be used to give modern spaces a fresh dimension when used in alcoves either side of a fireplace in a 1960s' retro-styled living room.

▸ Textured papers provide a wall with ready-made surface decoration. Experiment with the various matt and shiny surfaces on offer or the revival ranges of Lincrusta and Anaglypta, which can be painted over in a colour of your choice.

◄ Shadowy grey on white stripes give this wall a slightly aged and understated feel, an effect that would work well in a bedroom or living space where a calming atmosphere was needed.

► This subtly banded wallpaper has been used sideways so that the lines run vertically, giving the walls a blurred rib effect that is gentle and easy on the eye.

cladding

Cladding comes in plenty of guises and to suit all tastes and styles, from the rustic materials of wood and stone to Verner Panton's injection-moulded plastic bubble panels in glorious Technicolor.

Wood is perhaps the most commonly used form of cladding, and wood panelling is an interesting alternative to replastering if your walls are in need of an overhaul. Panelling is surprisingly versatile, and can be used in a variety of decorative ways. You can re-create the decorative effect of eighteenth-century panelling by fixing edge mouldings onto the walls in rectangles and then painting them. Fill the centre of the panels with a high-grade ply that can also be painted, and if you are using gloss paint apply it with a sponge roller for a smoother finish. For a neo-classical look, pick out the mouldings in white, and paint the wall in a pale shade of grey-lilac with the panels in a darker shade of lilac. Alternatively, cover the ply panels with silk or satin for a luxurious effect, or stick large mirror tiles to the panels to enhance the sense of space and provide a modern twist.

Tongue-and-groove panelling gives a room an old-world, country atmosphere, but also has its place in modern interiors. Traditionally used vertically, it gains a fresher edge when applied horizontally and has the added benefit of giving a narrow room a sense of width. Thin, inch-wide strips of wood attached to a ply base about an inch apart create a ribbed effect with a slightly retro feel that works well in modern homes. Stain the wood dark brown or Jacobean black to make it more contemporary.

Stone cladding can be used to create a variety of looks. Marble has a cool, sophisticated feel, while rough stones set in mortar will bring to mind a roaring fire in an alpine chalet. Stone tiles for walls are much thinner than stone floor tiles, to reduce the amount of weight on the wall, and they can be used just about anywhere. Marble and limestone are luxurious, versatile materials and

▲ An alcove has been covered with a faux shag-pile fur to create a luxurious, tactile bedhead wall.

▸ Strips of laminated wood line this arched connecting corridor. The addition of a tube light halfway up the wall carries through the light and airy quality of the living space.

▸ (overleaf) Natural coloured linen clads the walls in this subtly formal living room. The crisp white ceiling, coving and fireplace along with accents of black keep the colours clean and sophisticated.

can be stunning additions to both the kitchen and bathroom. However, they are both quite porous and have a tendency to stain, which you will need to consider before deciding to use them throughout the kitchen.

Granite comes in a large variety of colours, from deepest black through to green and blue. Some granite contains chips of quartz and is highly reflective when polished, which gives the stone a glitzy, glittery surface. For a cool, understated effect try using unpolished granite – its matt black surface is incredibly durable and can look quite amazing covering walls in a modern bathroom.

Slate is another popular stone cladding, which is cheaper than granite and comes in a range of colours from rusty red through to purple, green and blue-black. Use it with a sawn, riven finish in matt black to clad walls and floors in a bathroom or shower room and combine with chrome fittings. Stone comes in a variety of finishes, so contrast smooth surfaces with ribbed, chipped or pitted textured surfaces that are both beautiful to look at and to touch.

Leather wall hangings were the precursor to wallpaper, and were first introduced to Europe in the eleventh century by the Islamic peoples of North Africa. These wallcoverings were highly decorative, with decoration introduced with embossed and gilded surfaces. The surfaces featured large foliage-based patterns and although they were expensive, they were very strong and finished with a thick yellow varnish that made them resistant to dirt. Leather then became much less popular in the mid-seventeenth century when the arrival of wallpaper and silks from China prompted a fashionable preference for lighter decoration.

Recently leather and suede have become popular again through their extensive use in clubs and hotels. Walls are clad with padded panels of suede in rich, saturated colours. The

▲ (top) Thin strips of pine have been pinned to boarded walls to create a ribbed surface.

▲ (above) Cork tiles can be left untreated in a 1970s' style to make the most of their natural warmth. Alternatively, try some coloured cork tiles or treat plain ones with water-based washes.

► Bands of horizontal teak cladding accentuate the long, low dimensions of this room and also create a focal point around the fireplace.

look is warm, moody and very luxurious. Adapt the style for your home and use leather to cover a wall in a corner of a large room in order to create a place to relax in the evenings. Add a modern chrome chandelier, dark wood furniture and a boxy, low-level, suede seating-unit. For a more 'sci-fi' look, cover walls with white padded button-backed leather.

The 1950s saw the birth of the prefabricated home with its classic open-plan interiors, and this style gave rise to many more types of cladding. Designers and architects inspired by the Modern Movement wanted spaces that were natural looking, airy and inviting, and wood, stone and natural fibres such as hessian (burlap) and cork became very popular.

Advances in technology meant that man-made materials such as laminates were also used to cover walls. Available in a range of colours and patterns, they were also cheap and easy to apply. Laminates and wood veneers are good materials to use on curved surfaces because they are very flexible and can be simply glued in place. Polystyrene ceiling tiles, possibly the cheapest form of cladding available, can look surprisingly stylish: see the project on p112 for ideas.

Loft conversions gave rise to a whole range of cladding with cheap materials such as fibreboard used to cover breeze-block walls to give stark interiors a warmer appearance. Glass and sheet metal are still used extensively to clad walls in hallways, living spaces and bathrooms and are a reminder of these buildings' industrial pasts. Aluminium panels work well on kitchen walls in place of tiles, while highly reflective glass cladding backed with coloured enamel is an excellent material to use in bathrooms with no natural light. Sandblasted or etched glass is often used to build dividing walls as it offers a degree of privacy while still allowing light to diffuse into the space. These same qualities make it ideal for use in narrow corridors and entrances.

▲ Chocolate leather panels provide a luxurious headboard in this masculine bedroom.

▶ Plush, dove-grey velvet panels combine with a luxurious silk bedspread and creamy drapes to create a glamorous room reminiscent of a 1950s' film set.

▼ The curving sweep of this stairway has been given a more dramatic element with the use of sultry red suede panels on the walls. A matching carpet and an ornate chandelier enhance the effect.

Wall-Mounted Polystyrene Tiles

This project is quick, effective and requires no level of technical expertise. Polystyrene tiles are usually stuck to the ceiling but here they are used to create a simple and effective cladding for walls. Rather than butting them up close together, they are positioned to create a grid pattern. Paint the wall underneath a dark shade of grey and then paint the tiles a paler shade to enhance the relief effect. Experiment with different scales of tile and different shapes. Ornately patterned polystyrene ceiling roses could be butted up together to cover an entire wall. For a stunning monochromatic colour scheme, use Jasperware black as a basecoat.

When you are painting polystyrene tiles always use matt emulsion, as gloss or oil-based paints will melt them. Used in children's rooms, brightly coloured squares stuck to the wall can be used to pin up their latest paintings, photographs or postcards.

Tools & materials

MATT EMULSION BASECOAT

LIGHTER SHADE OF MATT EMULSION

POLYSTYRENE TILES

EMULSION BRUSHES

SPIRIT LEVEL

PENCIL

ADHESIVE

CARDBOARD TEMPLATE

CRAFT KNIFE

STEEL RULER

Method

1. First paint your wall with the darker matt emulsion and leave to dry.
2. Paint each of the polystyrene wall tiles with the lighter matt emulsion. Each tile will probably need two coats. Make sure that you have painted all the edges too.
3. Using the spirit level and starting in the centre at the top of the room and working down and outwards mark the position of your first tile using the pencil.
4. Following the manufacturer's instructions apply the adhesive to the tile and stick to the wall. Use a template to measure the distance between each tile (see p114).
5. Cut tiles to fit skirting (base board) and ends of walls using a craft knife and steel ruler, then paint the raw edge and stick to the wall as before.

◄ (step 2) Paint each of the polystyrene wall tiles with the lighter matt emulsion.

▲ (step 4) Use a template to accurately position the polystyrene tiles. To create the template, cut out a square of thick card the size of the tile in the centre and cut out from the cardboard frame the preferred spacing between each tile.

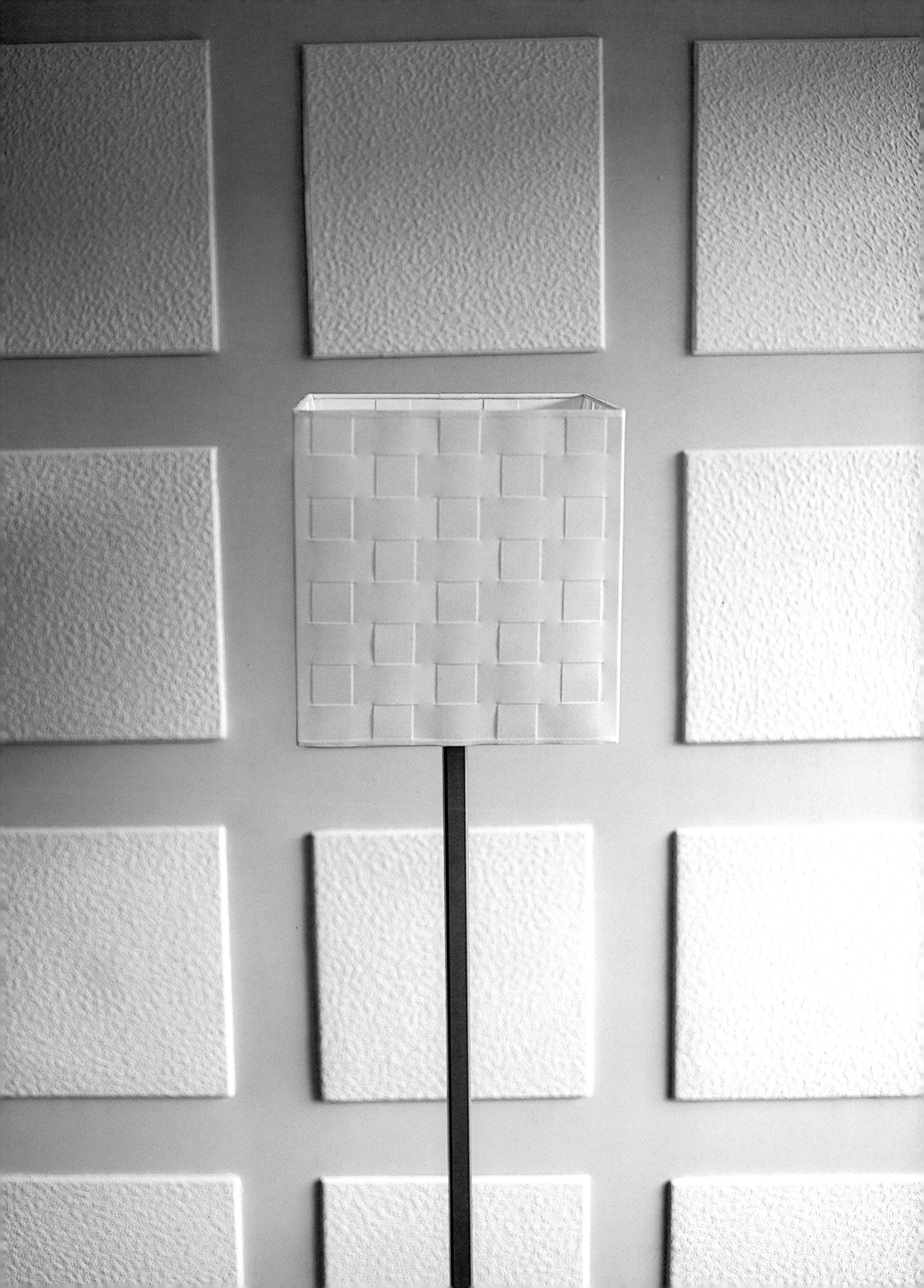

colour

Colour is a magical tool that can transform a room, shortening or widening its dimensions, creating a sense of space or intimacy and imparting a cool or warm atmosphere. The colour of the walls in a room sets its tone and is a highly personal choice: we are drawn to certain shades and abhore others. Colour triggers memories and associations for us and we only have to look at the way we describe colour to understand this: tangerine orange and Wedgwood blue, for example, are shades that can be identified with no problem at all.

▲ Sky-blue walls create a peaceful atmosphere and give rooms a fresh and calming quality. Silver, chrome and mirrored surfaces work particularly well with this shade of blue.

► A deep shade of plum gives this bedroom a warm and seductive air and the use of metallic paint on the woodwork and ceiling struts gives it a glamorous edge. More shades of purple are picked up in the large picture over the bed and in the bedlinen to create a coherent look.

Francis Ching says in his book, *Interior Design Illustrated*, 'There is no such thing as a good or bad colour. Some colours are just in or out of fashion at a given time.' Fashion has considerable influence on how we use colour. The emergence of synthetic pigments during the Industrial Revolution freed up the production process and allowed Victorians to revel in the use of different shades, while the minimalist backlash saw a rejection of colour in favour of monochromatic, mercilessly white interiors.

When choosing colour there are various elements to consider. What will the room be used for? What kind of atmosphere are you planning to create? What size is the room? And perhaps most important of all, what kind of light is available? Light is crucial: without light there is no colour. The purest light is white light: the sunlight at midday will show colours in their true shade. Light coming from a northerly direction will have a blue tint, while light from a southerly direction will be more yellow. This means that the same paint can look totally different depending on where it is used.

Artificial lights will also influence how we see colour, and different types of artificial lighting will produce different effects. Halogen light can flatten and bleach colour, while fluorescents come in many shades but tend to neutralize colour, and tungsten lights give off a yellow cast. This makes it important to check how your chosen shade appears under different lighting conditions. The simplest way is to paint good-sized patches onto the walls of your room. Dot the patches around the room and observe how the colour looks throughout the day.

Interiors are rarely made up of a single colour and all the elements of a room need to work together to form a coherent colour scheme. Colour schemes tend to divide into two types – contrasting and harmonizing. Contrasting schemes use vibrant and varied colours, while harmonizing schemes use colours that are tonally related. Because of this, contrasting schemes tend to be more energetic and visually stimulating, while harmonizing schemes create a calming and relaxing atmosphere and as a result they are particularly suitable for bedrooms and bathrooms.

When you are choosing colour for a room, start with swatches that match the items you will be putting there, such as a blue sofa, a dark wood sideboard or a brick-red rug. Decide what kind of scheme – contrasting or harmonizing – you would like and build a colour palette around the items that you already have.

white on white

Technically, white is a non-colour. It absorbs all the colours in the spectrum, from red through to violet, and reflects none, which is what makes it appear colourless. But take a closer look around you and you will see that white does not come in a single shade. Look at any paint chart and there will be multiple tones and hues to choose from, each slightly different but essentially white: snow-white, chalk-white, ivory, cream, milk-white, oyster-white, off-white, bone-white, brilliant white, lime-white – the list is endless.

Using a white colour scheme is often viewed as a cop-out and an easy option, but it is not as simple as it may seem. White interiors can be harsh and unforgiving – use too much and you could end up with snow-blindness on a sunny day. If you try blending cream woodwork with brilliant white walls it can look like something has gone wrong – the batch of paint used on the woodwork will appeared to have discoloured and yellowed.

But white is also a positive colour to use. It can visually enlarge a room, and it reflects light, intensifying and making the most of even weak sunshine on a winter's day. Don't underestimate the effect colour can have on your mood: white walls look clean and fresh and a bright and pure-looking room can help lift your spirits.

The many types of white can be broken into two groups, cool whites and warm whites. Cool whites have a grey, blue or even silver tone to them and are effective in rustic-style environments as they lend a cool, aged feel to walls. Warm whites have hints of yellow, pink and beige in them and create a soft, gentle effect in a room. Bear in mind the direction your room faces: use a creamy white in a north-facing room, and the yellow or pink tones will warm the cool blue light. Conversely, a south-facing room receives a much more yellow light, so can take a white in a blue-grey tone.

Think about the finish, too. White lacquer is highly reflective and works well in high-tech or very modern rooms but is a hard and unrelenting

▸ A living room for immaculately tidy purists – even the books have been covered with white paper. The walls, the door and the floor are flat and uniform, so attention focuses on the carefully placed furnishings and accessories.

surface that will show any imperfections. The soft, more forgiving sheen of eggshell works better on woodwork with period detailing and sits well with creamy whites. In an all-white colour scheme contrasting textures help to make the style work. For instance, cool matt white walls can be softened with bare woodwork that has been washed with a grey-white. A roughly plastered wall painted in a creamy tone can be freshened up with crisp white linen curtains and lace panels.

Certain paint techniques lend themselves to a white colour scheme and can help to make it less severe by adding texture, depth and pattern. Limewash and whitewash will give walls a soft, cloudy finish with a chalky colour. Limewash is not very white in its natural state, but can be made whiter with the addition of a white pigment, which will also help to make it more opaque. Natural wood can sometimes look raw against a white backdrop, so whitewashing, liming or using white wax will bring out the grain and give it a more mellow, timeworn finish.

Plaster finishes look beautiful coloured white. For rubbed-back or distressed plaster use tones of pure snowdrop-white over pale grey or, for a warmer effect, try creamy white on yellow. Stained with a dirty white, these finishes will look as if they have been there for hundreds of years. White crackle-varnish over a warm grey base can be used on skirting (base boards) and panelling to add an element of texture and variety to flat painted walls and will also help to define the walls' edges.

Black and white is a classic combination that is striking and powerful and can be used in a dining room for a formal atmosphere. If the contrast is too harsh, then think in terms of a black-and-white photo, where the effect is grainy, tonal and not so stark. Harsh colour combinations are easily softened by introducing mid-tones to link the two extremes. A white ceiling and Jacobean-black floorboards can be softened by using a pale grey on the walls. Pull it together with a combination of black, grey and white accessories.

▲ Panelled white walls create a soothing backdrop for the framed pictures in this bedroom. Textured cushions and linen add a tactile element to the interior.

▲ White walls combined with dark wooden steps and handrail enhance the dramatic sweep of this staircase.

► A heavy layer of crackling has been used to give this tongue-and-groove panelling a distressed look, and also adds textural interest to an all-white colour scheme.

Shadow Mural

Painting your own mural is an effective way of decorating a wall and is cheaper than buying a large work of art. Keep it simple by sticking to natural forms or abstract geometric patterns. This project was inspired by the decorative paintings of birch trees by Gustav Klimt. The simplest way of doing this is to project a picture of winter trees onto the wall, trace around it and then paint it in.

If you don't have a projector you can enlarge the image on a photocopier and create a stencil to trace around. If you use this method make sure that you overlap branches so that each section flows into the other and there are no obvious gaps. Choose subtle colours and restrict the palette to three to five colours. Shades of grey and white or tones of eau-de-nil work well.

Tools & materials

WHITE MATT EMULSION BASECOAT
PROJECTOR (IF USING THIS METHOD)
PENCIL
SLIDE OR PHOTO OF BARE TREES TO ENLARGE
TRACING PAPER
LARGE SHEET OF CARD FOR STENCIL
CRAFT KNIFE
CUTTING MAT
LOW-TACK MASKING TAPE
SPIRIT LEVEL
RULER
THREE LIGHT SHADES OF MATT EMULSION
EMULSION BRUSHES IN VARIOUS WIDTHS
MATT ACRYLIC VARNISH AND BRUSH (OPTIONAL)

Method

1. Paint the wall with the matt white emulsion basecoat and leave to dry.
2. (Projector method) Project the image onto the wall, adjusting it as necessary to get the right size. Using a pencil, trace around the trunks and branches of the trees. (Go to step 5.)
2. (Stencil method) Enlarge the image on a photocopier to around A0 size (91.5 x 127cm/36 x 50in) so that it is large enough for the wall. You may need to do this in sections, which can then be taped together, so that it is big enough. You will only need four or five trees that can be repeated along the wall to create a large panel.
3. Trace the image and transfer it onto a large sheet of card. Using a craft knife and cutting mat, cut out the tree trunks and branches to create a stencil.
4. Starting in the centre of the area you want to cover with the mural, tape the stencil to the wall, using a spirit level and ruler to make sure it is straight, and trace around the lines of the stencil with a pencil. Repeat, moving the stencil along, until you have filled the panel.
5. Paint in the background colour in a pale grey that is darker than the wall. Then paint in the trees using a fine emulsion brush and a darker grey emulsion to make them stand out. Pay attention to overlapping branches, making sure some go over others, and paint accordingly. Allow to dry completely before moving on to the next shade of emulsion.
6. If you want to protect the mural, cover it with a coat of matt acrylic varnish once the paint has dried.

Tip

▸ There are many alternatives for images for such a project: other ideas are abstract patterns, leaf images or an outline of grasses.

For more information on stencilling techniques see p29.

◂ (step 4) Trace around your stencil using a pencil. Repeat until you have filled the panel.

▸ (step 5) First of all paint in the background colour in a pale grey that is darker than the wall. Then paint in the trees using a fine emulsion brush and a darker grey emulsion to make them stand out.

neutrals

Designers have long understood the benefits of decorating a room with a neutral palette. A colour known as drab, an indeterminate beige-blue-grey colour, was the mainstay of eighteenth-century interiors and has recently experienced a revival. Like most neutrals it has a calming effect and flatters architectural details.

Neutral schemes make excellent backdrops for stunning pieces of furniture. Put a rosewood sideboard against caramel-coloured walls and see how the rich patina of the wood is enhanced. Similarly, a limestone-coloured wall will flatter the cool qualities and subtle veining of a marble bust or fire surround.

You can take a neutral colour scheme in two directions – the pale and interesting route or the darker, bitter-chocolate-coloured route. The darker scheme will create a cosier, more clubby atmosphere that is warm and inviting. Conversely, a scheme based on pale grey walls, white slipcovers and natural rush matting will make the most of available light and will create an airy feel reminiscent of Scandinavian interiors. This paler scheme is suited to rooms used during the day.

Consider the texture of neutral colours as this affects how you perceive a shade. A gloss paint or silk fabric will look different from a flat-painted surface or a slubby wool material of the same colour. Because one surface reflects light and the other absorbs it, they will appear to be different shades. An interplay of both kinds of surface, textured and smooth, is needed.

Neutrals are excellent for paint effects. The colours are flexible and can be used together without fear of clashing, which allows you to build up layers of broken colour to create a subtle wall finish with depth. Stone blocking and stone paint effects lend themselves to this colour scheme. A stone wall effect (see p34) in mellow sandstone tones makes a structured backdrop for a hallway. For a more geometric, abstract stone-effect use masking tape to create a grid pattern on the walls. Make each slab quite large as this helps to enhance the size of the

▸ Painting your walls in a neutral shade allows you to play with colour elsewhere in the room. Here the walls have been painted in a light khaki and the accents of citrine used in the furnishings uplift the colour scheme and draw the observer in.

▾ A neutral grey-purple tone has been used on the walls in this bathroom. Contrasting with the white ceiling and bath, the overall effect is confident and sophisticated with a definite French influence.

room. Rag or sponge the wall with up to four layers of neutral-coloured glazes, such as those that match the soft, creamy tones of natural limestone.

For a more abstract take on stone blocking, paint a basecoat on the wall of a pale beige colour and then criss-cross the walls with low-tack masking tape so that they intersect at angles to make different scales of rectangles, triangles, squares and rhomboids in a network of geometric shapes. Using a roller, paint over with a darker shade of beige, leave to dry, and then peel off the tape to reveal a geometric-patterned wall panel. This can add interest to alcoves, a bare wall or even two facing walls in a study.

Neutrals contain more than one pigment and it is this combination that gives them a grey, pink or yellow cast. This makes them complex colours, revealing different properties at different times of the day. Colourwashing works well with a neutral palette for this reason, but when selecting shades, stick to tones in the same family. For example, if you want to colourwash a wall with cool neutrals, use shades that have a grey tint. Rather than working on white, paint a basecoat of a pale grey and then apply glazes on top. For a really subtle effect, start with the lightest shade, work through the mid-tones and then finish with a light wash of the darkest colour in your palette.

More textural paint effects also suit a neutral colour scheme. Use stippling for gentle texture that is only noticeable close up. Cord paint is a simple way of adding texture to your walls. This specialist paint is rollered over a similar-coloured basecoat and the cord texture is achieved by dragging through the wet paint with a stiff, short-bristled brush. Choose soft camel shades and use with deep skirting boards (base boards) stained chocolate brown. Temper this powerful look with white ceilings.

Similar in principle to cord paint, combing (see p27) can be effective on walls. Create a retro look with mock pine panelling, or for a cooler, more sophisticated approach, use blue-tinted neutrals to create the effect of walls lined with moiré silk (see p39).

▲ This geometric wallpaper by Anya Larkin at Donghia is covered in an aluminium-based paint and painted with multicoloured stripes. It picks up on the other square design forms.

▶ This wall is split subtly in half, with the lower part painted a slightly deeper shade than the upper section. This helps to focus the eye on the antique sofa that has been given a modern facelift with a new cover of plain, drab-coloured cotton.

▼ Despite the grand proportions of this entrance hall, the colour scheme gives it an inviting quality. If white walls and a black-and-white chequered floor had been used, the effect would have been too cold.

Pompadour Pink Colour Dragging

Dragging creates a striated effect that allows the base colour to show through a softly tinted glaze. Here the technique has been used to decorate the wall behind a headboard for an elegant, feminine effect in a bedroom. The dragging technique is derived from wood graining (see p32), and was traditionally done using a thick, dark glaze. The transparent glazes of today, however, allow us to introduce more subtle shades. Oil-based glazes are the easiest to work with because they take longer to dry, which means the surface is workable for longer. Dragging is best used on flat surfaces as the vertical lines and glossy nature of the glaze highlight any uneven patches.

Tools & materials

EGGSHELL BASECOAT

OIL-BASED GLAZE

ARTIST'S OIL COLOUR TO TINT GLAZE

WHITE SPIRIT

CONTAINER FOR MIXING GLAZE

STANDARD PAINTBRUSHES

FOAM ROLLER AND TRAY

DRAGGING BRUSH

RAG

CLEAR MATT ACRYLIC VARNISH AND BRUSH

Method

1. Paint the eggshell basecoat and allow to dry.
2. Tint the oil-based glaze with the artist's oil colour, mixing to the desired shade. Stir in white spirit drop by drop until the glaze is slightly thinner than single cream.
3. Apply the glaze to the basecoat using a paintbrush or roller. Work up and down and across for even coverage.
4. Using the dragging brush, start from the top and drag down the length of the wall in one long, uninterrupted stroke (see below). If one stroke is impossible then brush downward from the top as far as possible and then from the bottom upward. Brush out the strokes at the end of each drag so they meet subtly in the middle. For a rougher effect, go over the brushstrokes again.
5. Wipe the dragging brush on a rag to keep it clean and prevent clogging.
6. Repeat until the entire surface has been dragged. Allow the glaze to dry and then apply a protective coat of clear matt acrylic varnish.

Tips

▸ This technique is hard to do well over a large area because it is difficult to keep the lines straight. Restrict it to one wall only or use on panelling and skirting (base boards). For larger areas, drag downward and then across for a looser checked look.

▸ A pale-tinted glaze applied over a darker base creates a more modern effect.

▸ If you are working on a large area then only glaze a metre at a time, working section by section.

For more information on dragging techniques see p25.

brilliants

If you want a room to have pace and energy, paint it in a glorious, bright colour. It really is as simple as that. However, there is a real art to using pure strong colour – so whatever you do, don't choose a brilliant colour for your walls without thinking it through. Once you have considered exactly how it will work, you may conclude that shocking pink just isn't for you.

When looking at strong colour it is natural to think of warmer climes: the white-and-blue combination typical of Greece; the vibrant, almost super-real, colours of Indian Hindu temples; and the turquoise, pink, yellow and orange combinations of Mexico. Brilliant colours work particularly well in hotter countries because the light is brighter and whiter than in the northern hemisphere. This does not mean that those in the north have to discount or avoid strong colour; you only have to look back to the 1960s when clashing orange, pink and yellow were the height of fashion to realize that strong colour can be used the world over.

To understand how strong colour can be used, it is worth looking at the work of Luis Barragán, most notably the house and stud farm stables that he designed for the San Cristobal Estate, Mexico City, in 1967–1968. Self-taught, he developed a very distinctive form of architecture: his work had the modern simplicity of Le Corbusier, but featured large planes of oscillating colour, almost certainly adopted from his surroundings in Mexico.

Barragán used colour in a simple way. Rather than mixing a collection of bright shades in an unco-ordinated mass of colour, he simply used one vibrant shade, often on a single wall, so that it dominated a room and set the mood. This is certainly the easiest way to use brilliant colour: start with a single shade and if you are nervous, confine it to just one wall. Then offset it with white, which will help to heighten its impact. You can also balance the strong colour by using it

▸ Flat colour in this brilliant violet-red shade would have been too intense, so this bedroom wall was painted with a base of plaster-pink matt emulsion and then sponged with a plum-coloured wash, then roughly softened with a long-haired brush. Touches of whiting were then rubbed into the topcoat for a streaky look.

elsewhere in the room. For example, if you have a shocking pink wall, white floor and ceiling and a white sofa, add some matching pink cushions and line bright pink or baby blue glassware along the mantelpiece to stimulate the eye and draw it around the room.

If you decide to seriously adopt the use of bright colours in your interiors, then do try to avoid using too much contrasting colour, such as bright yellow and purple, or green and red. The effect will be exciting and impart a feeling of energy but if you are living with it permanently, it can be too busy and overwhelming and leave you feeling restless and agitated.

Some colours work together better than others. When combining brilliant colours, look through books on global design for inspiration; certain pairings and combinations will recur, simply because they are so effective. Turquoise and aqua blues work well on walls and accents of orange, red and pink will sit happily with them. Combine stronger electric and ultramarine blues with touches of yellow or white to give a room an atmosphere that is fresh and clean but still upbeat. A splash of acid green is a less predictable shade to use with the blues and it will hold its own as long as there is plenty of white in the room too.

Perhaps the most startling and inviting range of brilliant colours to play with are the shades that start at red-orange and run through bright red and crimson, finishing at bubble-gum pink. These colours stand out, signifying excitement, danger and passion. We are drawn to them but they are not for the faint-hearted. Use red or orange where warmth is needed, but in small spaces confine them to one wall and contrast them with more natural shades. Bright pink works well alongside dashes of aqua and yellow; alternatively clash it with poppy red and vibrant orange for a full-on sexy atmosphere. Jewel-coloured emerald is tempered when combined

▲ (top) Medium-green is a strong base colour for this hallway, complemented by the surrounding subdued colours.

▲ (above) These crimson walls create a warm and sociable atmosphere in this casual dining area and also define the unusual shape of the pendant lamps hanging over the table.

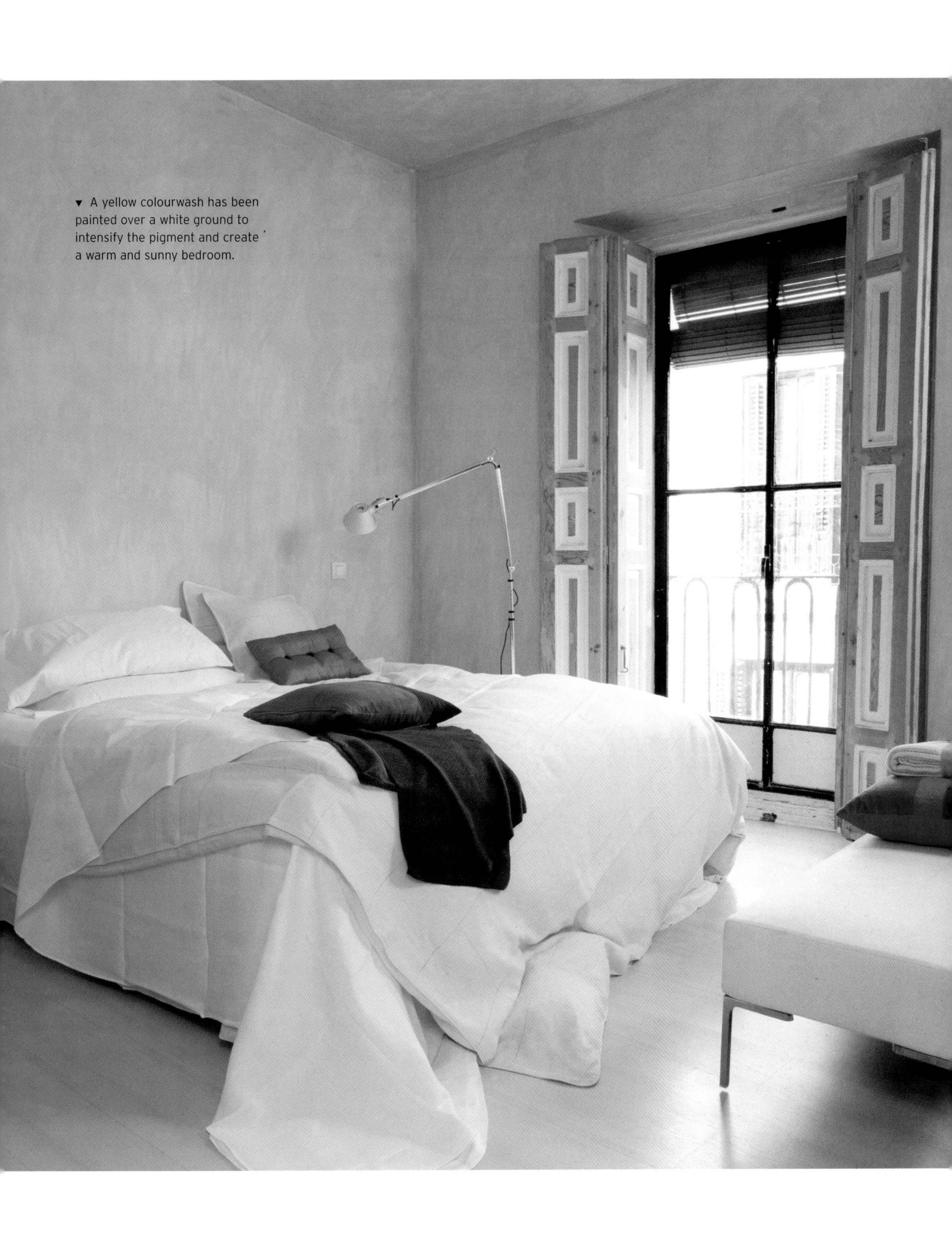

▼ A yellow colourwash has been painted over a white ground to intensify the pigment and create a warm and sunny bedroom.

with lime and peppermint. Try painting an entire wall emerald green and then adding a wide stripe of lime green at one end, flanked by thinner stripes of peppermint. The effect will be soothing but never dull.

When considering wall effects, colourwashing, the painting of thin washes of glaze over a coloured background (see p24), is an effective technique to use with brilliant colour, especially if you want a more rustic style and more depth than flat paint. A strong blue glaze washed over white will give you an intense hit of colour that looks as if it has just been brushed on and works well in country-style bedrooms with lots of beams. Limewashing (see p35), traditionally used to achieve a chalky white, subdued finish, is an excellent technique to use with intensely coloured pigments. Use fuchsia pink or bright blue for a powdery but very saturated matt finish that looks as if it has been built up over years. This works well painted over brick walls or rough, uneven plaster.

If you are drawn to bright colour but prefer to subdue it by giving it an aged look, then try using a mock plaster technique (see p38). Bear in mind that powder pigments are very strong, and always test the colour first on a scrap piece of board to avoid mistakes. If you want a paler shade, add more whiting, but make sure it is mixed in well so that you don't end up with a streak of white. This technique can be used on smooth walls or rough plaster and the wax finish makes it a very durable surface that is suitable for kitchens, bathrooms, hallways or anywhere that gets a lot of wear. For further inspiration, take a look at the Gloss Stencil project on p64. This uses a brilliant pink basecoat with a gloss stencil of the same colour for a modern injection of colour and pattern. Brilliant colour works well with a glossy finish as it brings to life the intensity of the colour. Experiment with brightly coloured gloss doors and use a foam roller for a brushmark-free finish.

▲ (top) This crimson wall is balanced with adjacent white walls, white flooring and furniture. This balancing technique allows the injection of a strong, energetic colour without completely overpowering the space.

▲ (above) The combined success of the myriad of colours shown here is heavily reliant on the sky-blue colour that highlights the alcove in the wall of this bedroom.

▶ The deep-orange panels bordering this deck ensure that it has a warm hue all year round and demonstrates that strong colour can be used outside, too.

Bridget Riley Striped Wall

This project was inspired by Bridget Riley's calming striped paintings of the early 1980s and, if you like stripes, it is an imaginative way to introduce colour into a room. If you use horizontal stripes it will enhance the feeling of width. Use a piece of striped fabric as a guide for the pattern, scaling up the bands to fit the wall. For a more subtle look, vary the widths of the bands. Using white in between coloured stripes will keep it looking fresh and prevent it from being too overpowering. Choose the colours from paint charts. For a soothing effect, select shades within the same colour family and for a more vibrant feel, add a hot contrasting colour to the selection.

Tools & materials

WHITE MATT EMULSION BASECOAT

RULER

SPIRIT LEVEL

PENCIL

LOW-TACK MASKING TAPE

THREE TO FIVE SHADES OF MATT EMULSION

EMULSION BRUSHES

SMALL ROLLERS AND TRAY

ARTIST'S BRUSH

Method

1. Paint the wall with the white matt emulsion basecoat and leave to dry completely.
2. Using the ruler and spirit level, mark the stripes on the wall with a pencil. Start halfway up the wall and measure stripes downward and upward from there.
3. Working with one colour at a time, use the low-tack masking tape to mask the edges of the stripes to be painted in the first colour. Then paint in the colour: for wide stripes use a roller and for thinner stripes use a good-quality emulsion brush (see below).
4. Leave the stripes to dry completely and then carefully remove the masking tape. If paint has bled or not filled to the edge use the artist's brush to make adjustments.
5. Repeat for the rest of the colours. Avoid leaving masking tape on the walls for more than a day as it can leave marks or even lift the basecoat colour.

▲ (step 2) Use a ruler and spirit level to make sure that your stripes are perfectly straight: draw them in lightly with a pencil.

► (step 3) Use low-tack masking tape to mask off each stripe as you paint it. Remove the tape carefully so as not to disturb the paint, and fill in any chips with a fine artist's brush.

deep & saturated colour

What do we mean when we refer to deep, saturated colours? These are the shades that are too intense to be called neutral, yet aren't brilliant because they don't leap off the wall and dazzle with their brightness. Deep, saturated colours are subtle, yet always make a strong statement. They are made up from many pigments and usually contain blue-grey tones, so are on the darker side of colour.

Deep, saturated colours can be cool or warm and include shades such as aubergine, peacock blue, fir green, burnt orange and claret. These colours can be wonderfully evocative and can be used to create a brooding interior with hidden depths or equally a mellow and inviting space that guests will feel at home in.

Colour preferences are very personal and it is best to choose combinations that you are drawn to, although this can in some cases be too limiting. If you haven't considered them before, experiment with darker colours – you may be surprised by the effect they have and how much you like them. Throughout the 1980s and 1990s, the trend was for spacious, light-filled, open-plan interiors. Yet the reality of living in these kinds of spaces is not always as good as it looks; as everything happens in the same room, you can't get away from the sounds of the rest of the household for a sense of privacy or even just a quiet read. Sometimes it is a relief to settle down in a small and cosy room to enjoy a peaceful moment. Saturated colours can be used to create this effect in a corner of a large room or to enrich the atmosphere of a smaller room.

As with most colours, the easiest way to use deep colour is to paint the walls a single field colour and then temper this with lighter woodwork and ceiling colours, in combination with a matching floor treatment. Alternatively, reject conventional rules and use the colour all over. It is only by trying different approaches that you will find one that works for you.

▸ Deep-chocolate brown and shades of white are a dramatic colour combination. The brown walls are used to frame the doorway to the white bathing area. The whites and other softer colours on the patchwork bedspread also lift the light-absorbing brown.

▾ Don't automatically avoid the use of deep colours, because they can create dramatic, intimate backdrops for collections of favourite objects. In this living room, a brown leather Mies Van Der Rohe Barcelona chair sits alongside a lava lamp and a collection of pottery.

If a room receives hardly any natural light it seems pointless trying to make it falsely bright and airy. Choose instead dark tones that look fabulous under electric light, such as ripe damson, deep Indian red or even rich yellow-ochre. Match your lighting to suit the scheme. A combination of candlelight and subtle uplighters will create deep shadows in corners, making furniture appear more statuesque than it actually is. People often look their best under this kind of light and against a backdrop of deep colour, which goes some way to explaining why there is a tradition for strong colour schemes in the dining room.

Many deep, saturated colours have a historical reference. The Victorians were keen on a rich maroon, while the Georgians used a deep, sludgy green that was popularized by the Adam brothers. Looking much further back, Pompeii red – a rich, warm and earthy colour – is still popular today. Many of the fashionable heritage colours fall within this range – among those developed by Farrow & Ball for the National Trust are Eating Room Red and Green Smoke. Alternatively, the Paint and Paper Library range designed by Nina Campbell and David Oliver includes Cassis, Olive Oil and Elizabethan Red.

Using saturated colour in an interior also provides you with the opportunity to use a rich and highly decorative range of paint effects. Wood graining (see p32) can be used to create the impression of mahogany panelling above or below a dado rail. Use a rich yellow-ochre or burnt red to complement the effect. Stain skirting boards (base boards) and doors (see p33) with a shade that matches the graining for a unified look.

If you have ornate cornices and a white wood or marble fire surround, then think about painting the walls a deep aubergine colour. A flat matt finish will look highly sophisticated and is the perfect foil for large paintings in ornate gold frames. In order to maximize the amount of light in the room, finish the wall with a glaze coat. The

▲ The saturated earth-brown paint in this space enhances the textured accessories and elegantly shaped wooden chairs in the foreground.

▶ An inky black wall makes a bold statement and focuses attention on the ornate marble fireplace, a quirky contrast to the modern setting.

▼ A deep slate colour has been used to paint the walls of this open-plan living space. It serves as a theatrical backdrop against which colourful abstract paintings and a sculpture are positioned.

sheen of this finish will then help to reflect light around the room without detracting from the intensity of the colour. Use a foam roller to avoid any visible brushstrokes.

Deep colours are also suitable for use with ageing techniques such as antiquing and gilding (see p31). Use a grey and a blue-brown glaze on a limewashed wall or woodwork for a finish with the colours and aged appearance of traditional Scandinavian interiors. New pine panelling can be made to look old with an ageing glaze made from raw umber and raw sienna (see p33). A rust effect is not traditionally used on walls, but a grid of rust panels on a smoky or chocolate-coloured background would make a stunning feature wall in a more modern home.

▲ Deep shades of red and pink work well with the stained wooden panelling and create a traditional style to the room.

◄ Dark, plain colours can highlight patterned elements. The delicate lacquer work on the chests is well defined by the contrasting dark olive shade of the walls in this room.

► The deep brown colour of the walls in this bedroom is an unexpected contrast to the traditional iron bedstead and the country style of the other features.

ΜΠΙΣΚΟΤΑ

style

Style is about creating a signature look. It isn't about slavishly copying an existing design but cherry-picking the best of what you like and making it your own. This chapter identifies four popular trends with their own techniques, colour palettes, textures and formats, which can be used as building blocks to create your own style.

▲ An all-white colour scheme is easy to live with and simple to furnish. Here the walls have been clad with horizontal tongue-and-groove to add texture and interest to the walls.

▶ The owner of this space has a sense of fun and a love of colour: rustic plastered walls finished in grey contrast with a vibrant pink window frame, a colourful mosaic floor and quirky furniture.

Cross-Cultural Style is about bringing ideas and techniques from around the globe into your home. Whether you love the rich spice colours of India, the hand-carved wooden panels and sculpture of southern Africa or the naivety of Eastern European folk art, it is possible to include these elements in your home without it looking like a theme park. For example, an old Indian doorframe with ornate carving could be backed with a mirror and hung against a wall painted in a pale Indian blue or warmer shades of saffron, giving a subtle flavour of Indian design.

The popularity of retro designs from the 1950s through to the 1970s looks set to stay, but Retro Style involves incorporating choice elements and authentic accessories rather than a complete historical recreation. Using retro-inspired wallpapers or colour is the easiest way of subtly introducing a period theme that is easy to live with. Alternatively, stick to plain shades on the walls and use patterned upholstery fabric that is typical of your chosen era to cover modern or period furniture.

A Modern Rustic style is the new interpretation of the country look and involves a pared-down approach to decorating, in which raw materials are left exposed and simple modern furniture integrates with the rural environment. This style, more than any of the others, is particularly suited to traditional wall treatments, which, as they form the structure of the room, will set the theme. Heavily distressed plaster, exposed beams, limewash, textured plaster finishes and exposed brick are all classic wall finishes used to create the Modern Rustic look. Ruthless editing is an important aspect of this style. Rooms need to be homely but spartan, walls are often left without pictures, clutter is banished to leave clear surfaces on which the odd item such as a bowl, a piece of driftwood or a collection of shells might be displayed.

The New Romantic style takes a very different approach, and highlights the trend for a more extravagant and decadent use of design. New romantic interiors are eclectic, typically mixing a rococo-style chair and distressed plasterwork with sumptuous fabrics. This is a style that allows you to experiment with more decorative techniques such as gilding ornate plasterwork or painting crackle finishes on wood to give an impression of age. The look is pretty, ultra-feminine and dedicated to the display of vintage treasures, whether inherited or discovered in boot sales and antique fairs.

cross-cultural style

It is all too easy to be inspired by the interiors of far-flung destinations. Bringing the look home and pulling it together with the same effect is a different matter, however, and requires strict editing. For this style, less is usually more, but that does not mean that you have to be ruthless. It is possible to combine items from all over the world and incorporate your favourite cross-cultural elements into your home. For success, aim for a unifying element, whether this is a colour or a basic range of materials.

If you are drawn to the style of the Orient, study its traditional elements. Japanese interiors are spare and make regular use of bamboo, wood and paper to create rooms that appear open and airy, even if the actual dimensions are on a small scale. In Thailand and Bali the approach tends to be more decorative, with ornately carved architectural details and furniture. Rattan and bamboo sliding screens act as moveable walls, encompassing the outside world or closing it off as desired. One way of interpreting this style at home is by using different vertical lengths of bamboo poles to clad the surface of a wall. This will create an illusion of height and the rich mellow tones will add warmth to the room.

Classic Eastern living is low level, and you can also add detail to skirting (base boards) with carved moulding or a rich lacquer finish so that there is something to catch the eye when sitting on the floor. The colour palette tends to be naturally inspired, with accents of rich red, gold and black.

In India, sensory stimulation abounds. From the beautiful palaces of Rajasthan to the high-octane kitsch of Bollywood movies, colours, textures and smells are intense. The arch is a key Indian architectural feature. Whether a doorway with a scalloped edge or a simple niche in the wall, these arches are often ornately decorated with swirling arabesques and floral patterns. Make a feature of a plain door by painting the outline of a scalloped arch around it in white on top of a rich but chalky

► A mural of an Indian goddess floating in the night sky has been used to add a decorative and slightly kitsch element to this alcove, where the goddess floats above a collection of Indian dolls.

▼ While the architectural details and ceiling decoration in this Indian home have an ornate formality, the blue-and-white colour scheme gives the room a calm, cool quality, ensuring it is the perfect place of retreat during the hottest part of the day.

earth colour. For a calming interior, use the distinctive pale blue of Jodhpur as the base colour of a room, with saris at the windows to add pattern and to diffuse the light.

The vast continent of Africa is home to a wide range of decorative styles. Moroccan interiors have richly patterned walls in bright colours, with cool tiled floors and intricate fabrics. Chased brass panels are used on doors and coloured glass lanterns hang from the ceiling. To re-interpret the Moorish influence at home, use filigree screens for lining walls or as shutters over windows. Use them to build temporary room dividers between a living and dining area, providing a little privacy but still allowing light and air to flow through the room.

The mud houses of South Africa are painted in fantastic earth and mineral colours. Graphic chevrons and abstract blocks of colour cover the walls and are as sophisticated and individual as a Missoni striped scarf. Nothing is wasted: bits of scrap metal and car parts are imbedded into the wall and a fork is used to create a combed texture in paint. Black and white are used to outline hand-drawn patterns with a haphazard, spontaneous feel. Bring elements of this into your home by combining a panel of zigzag lines in white, black, camel and rusty red with a collection of carved wooden sculptures. Display the sculptures on a rough wooden shelf in front of this abstract mural for an informal gallery.

Look at the colour combinations used in the once grand neo-classical buildings of Cuba. Aquamarine and shocking pink are used side by side and have a bleached quality from years of exposure to the sun. This level of intense colour all over a room can be overpowering, so try painting the walls white and then adding a hot pink rectangular panel on one wall, with a large square aquamarine panel on the adjacent wall. The colours will play off each other but the effect will be diffused by the white areas. If you do decide to use bright colour all over, paint the ceiling white so that

▲ Deep, firebrick red plaster walls give this room a theatrical element. The niche – topped with an arabesque and decorated with a gilded tree, sun and birds – intensifies the richness and provides all the decoration required.

▶ Reminiscent of Gauguin's Tahitian paintings, the walls in this room are clad with rush screening with a highly textured surface. A mirror frame of shells, a wooden bowl and the lush vegetation depicted in the fabric all enhance the natural theme.

▲ The simple design on this wall was made by scratching into wet plaster, an excellent method of adding three-dimensional pattern with no colour.

◄ A baked earth wall in India is decorated with the architectural outlines of windows. This idea is a useful template to give structure to a wall or to create the illusion of panelling.

► Roughly textured walls, simply painted in a terracotta and cream-tinted limewash, combine well with simple furnishings and the earthy quality of this South African interior.

it keeps the colour clean, and prevents the walls from being too overwhelming. Kitchens can usually take strong colour combinations as wall-mounted cupboards help to break up the space. Soften the colour by adding whiting or chalk powder to the mix to create a slightly bleached quality.

The adobe homes of Mexico are characterized by curved, bulging walls painted with vibrant colours. Walls are inset with blue and white tiles, and elaborately curled wrought-iron grilles cover windows. Try hanging similar grilles on the wall as an alternative decoration to framed pictures. Mexican colour combinations are exuberant – bright yellow, cobalt blue and turquoise are painted side by side. Painted borders run riot – abstract animals and flowers chase one another around alcoves, fireplaces, the edge of a room, or even around a large piece of furniture. To use colour in this way you need to forget your inhibitions and revel in its vibrancy.

retro style

Retro is a loose term that tends to apply to the styles of the 1950s, 1960s and 1970s, which have recently undergone a fashion revival. After the period of austerity during and after the Second World War, the 1950s saw the rise of a generation of consumers eager for new products for the home. The new ranges of paints, enamels, papers, panelling and laminates were a revelation after the shortages of the war. The consumer boom of the 1950s and 1960s and the growing middle class led to an enthusiastic market of DIYers who used their homes to reflect their status.

Houses became smaller and open plan with low ceilings and built-in furniture. Classic shades for interiors during the 1950s were salmon pink, pale blue, turquoise, black and yellow. The interest in science and confidence in technology led to the design of molecular-patterned wallpaper in 1951 and these scratchy black linear patterns on a pastel background seemed to typify the era. The design was often applied to walls as a paint effect, by working a patterned roller over the top of a pastel basecoat.

Wall treatments such as varnished wood, exposed brick and stone effects were popular, while wallpaper with images of fruit and vegetables or crockery was used extensively in the kitchen and still has an amusing appeal today. Floral wallpapers, particularly sprig patterns, were used predominantly in the bedroom, and spots and stripes were also fashionable. Black spots and stripes on a pastel-pink ground can create a startlingly graphic and sweetly nostalgic effect. Think about using them in a dressing room and live out all your secret 1950s starlet fantasies.

Advances in technology and the consumer boom led to a throwaway consumer mentality in the late 1950s, which grew into the Pop Art culture of the 1960s and had an enormous impact on design. Colour became more saturated, positively loud in comparison to the schemes of the previous decade, and pattern was scaled up to create bold designs. There was also a revival of Art Nouveau and Art

▲ If you are creating a retro interior, use colours and designs in keeping with the era, such as this sludgy green-yellow scheme reminiscent of a 1960s' home.

▶ The retro revival has led to an explosion in 1960s- and 1970s-inspired wallpapers. This abstract print is the ideal backdrop for a collection of furniture ranging in style from the 1950s to the present day.

Deco style, with gold and black embossed Art Deco motifs used on walls and ceilings, both at home and in fashionable stores such as Biba in London.

Op Art, pioneered by artist Bridget Riley in Britain, also had a massive impact on design, generating an explosion of graphic, swirling patterns that were applied to walls everywhere. The psychedelic style of the 1970s merely carried Op Art to extremes. Neon lights and paints were combined with large-scale graphics and took over walls and entire room schemes. There was no longer any concept of boundaries: designs that started at floor level blazed a trail up the wall, cutting across corners at angles, and eventually working their way up onto the ceiling. At the same time, a reaction against mass production and growing ecological concerns led to the Flower Power counterculture, in which decorating the home was not about status but about making a political statement of allegiance to one group or another.

The hippie ethos was responsible for introducing ethnic products to interiors such as carvings, wall hangings and textiles from around the world, especially India. Authentic colour combinations for a 1970s room scheme include purple, orange, yellow, turquoise and any shade of brown. Use them all together or on their own, but the more colour clashes the better. If you have a 1960s or 1970s dining suite, decorate the dining area with wide, multicoloured rainbow stripes that curve and bend their way around the room, combining strong colours with huge, bold pattern in one scheme.

Some of the best places to look for inspiration for a 1960s- or 1970s-style interior are cult films such as Barbarella and 2001: A Space Odyssey, or alternatively simply consult decorating manuals of the time, easily found in secondhand book shops. A quick browse through one of these may inspire you with brown diagonal stripes painted across one wall in a bedroom, a rainbow and cloud mural in a bathroom, tangerine-coloured hallways or pine panelling galore.

▸ Wallpaper with an Art Nouveau design injects bold pattern and colour into this dining room. Furniture from the 1960s creates an eclectic mix of styles with a modern statement.

▾ Cladding was popular from the 1950s and reached its height in the 1970s. Here, a chequerboard of different-coloured woods clads the walls of this dining room.

Wood Panelling

Wood cladding gives a room a warm and cosy feel. Use it to create an atmospheric dining room or home office. Large planks of overlapping pine will evoke the feel of a Nordic chalet, but for an authentic retro effect, use wood veneers in rich, dark shades of oak, teak, rosewood and mahogany. Experiment with different shapes and sizes of veneer. Long horizontal floorboard-sized strips will help to add width to a room, squares will give a more uniform effect, and vertical planks will add height.

Laminate flooring can also be used to clad walls but it doesn't have the texture and authenticity of wood veneers. If you are using laminate floorboards follow steps 1–3 and then use nail-free glue to stick each laminate board onto the mdf, interlocking each one as you go. Allow the glue to dry after the first three rows before adding any more boards, so that they don't slip off when you add further rows.

Tools & materials

BATONS

JIGSAW

DRILL

RAWL PLUGS

MASONRY SCREWS

SCREWDRIVER

MDF BOARDS

WOOD FILLER

MEDIUM-GRADE SANDPAPER

KNIFE

STEEL RULER

SHEETS OF WOOD VENEER

OR LAMINATE FLOORING

VENEER GLUE STRIPS

SATIN ACRYLIC VARNISH

BRUSH OR WHITE WAX

CLOTH TO SEAL WOOD

Method

1. Start by fixing the batons to the wall in a grid pattern. Use a jigsaw to cut the batons to length and screw them to the wall using a drill, masonry screws and appropriate rawl plugs at intervals of no more than 30cm (12in) apart to form a firm base.
2. Attach the mdf boards to the batons with screws, making sure the screws are recessed below the surface of the boards and then filled with wood filler and sanded smooth.
3. If you are using veneer, cut it into squares or board-length strips with a knife and steel ruler, depending on the pattern you want.
4. Following the manufacturer's instructions, use veneer glue strips to attach the veneer pieces to the mdf. Make sure you smooth them down, paying particular attention to sticking down the edges. Alternatively, lay the laminate flooring in the same way.
5. Allow the glue to cure for a couple of hours and then finish with satin acrylic varnish or white wax to seal the wood and bring up the grain.

21

◂ (step 1) Batons are attached to the walls to provide a sturdy framework.

◂ (step 2) The mdf boards are then attached to the batons. This gives a firm and level surface.

◂ (step 4) The veneer strips are attached to the mdf with veneer glue strips: each one should be smoothed down carefully. Alternatively, if using laminate flooring, attach this to the wall. Use a variety of veneers or laminates to create a rich and varied surface.

21

modern rustic

The enduring popularity of country style is probably due in large part to its evocation of an idealized – and largely imaginary – notion of the country lifestyle. Even hardened urbanites cannot ignore its charms and want to re-create that sense of rural idyll in their homes. But today's interpretation of the rural retreat no longer features dried flowers and cluttered pine dressers. The new rustic style has evolved out of the modern movement, and draws on the stripped-back minimalism that has appeared in so many city dwellings, with a slightly less rigorous approach. It could be said to mirror the reaction of the Arts and Crafts movement to the overly decorative and industrialized interiors of the Victorian era in its approach to materials and decoration.

Walls play a large and important role in creating the Modern Rustic look. Their treatment can create that air of wanton neglect that suggests the interior was left just as it was discovered. Bare brick is left exposed or washed with a coat of lime; stone and mortar walls are offset with stripped wood sealed with a coat of wax or oil; and plaster is left in a natural, unfinished state with the warm, earth-colour acting as the perfect backdrop for a splash of colour or an ornate family heirloom.

Modern Rustic utilizes all the conveniences and comforts of contemporary living such as heating, running water and electricity, but is more in touch with nature. Many outhouses and barn conversions have double-height windows stretching from the ground to the apex of a gable, which flood the space inside with light and let in as much of nature as possible. Small, heat-conserving windows are rejected, because we no longer have to rely on a single fire to heat the house.

The Modern Rustic style appreciates the raw structure of a building and natural materials such as stone are used to clad the walls. If you want a cool, contemplative interior, smooth creamy limestone will create a luxurious yet almost church-like atmosphere. Irregular blocks of stone and

▲ (top) Whitewashed walls, exposed beams and a black Aga, combined with a lack of fussy decoration, give this kitchen a fresh, rural look.

▲ (above) The wooden panelling on the wall of this room has been stripped of paint and simply waxed to create a warm modern atmosphere, against which a bench sofa has been placed.

▶ This sunny hallway has a relaxed and rustic feel, created by the rough plastered walls decorated with plaster tondos, flagstone flooring and worn painted furniture.

▶ The creamy, colourwashed walls in this large living space are unadorned apart from the crystal wall sconces. The overall atmosphere is one of relaxed country grandeur.

mortar recall more humble dwellings, while uniformly shaped stone blocks bring to mind grand hunting lodges and castles.

Plaster is an important material in the Modern Rustic interior. Strip back wallpaper to find the previous incarnations of the house. If you are lucky enough to find patches of a colour you like, experiment with sanding it back to get rid of any loose material and leave it as a decorative reminder of the past. Don't try to hide old, cracking plaster but enhance it with a wash of chalky white paint or use a colour glaze to sit in the cracks and emphasize the crazed pattern, like a natural form of crackle glaze. Plaster finishes are suited to rooms with low ceilings as plaster is softer and less imposing than bare brick or stone, both of which can look heavy. Experiment with distressed or rough plasters finishes (see pp36 and 37). Rubbed-back plaster (see p37) will give a subtler, aged look.

Tongue-and-groove cladding, usually made from pine, was used to insulate walls and conceal a rough finish. Introduce it to a room that has no remarkable features, and position it so that it finishes three-quarters of the way up the wall to create a display ledge that can be used to stand finds such as stones and sun-bleached wood. Wooden panelling comes in many guises: shiplap is reminiscent of basic shacks found in the Wild West; walls made with logs immediately evoke the cool climes of Scandinavia; and full-height wainscoting with linen-fold carving conjures up the image of medieval dining halls.

When creating a Modern Rustic interior, aim for a simple, pared-down finish that transcends fashion. Your wall should be the perfect foil to both a modern glass table and a scrubbed-pine table and bench. Contrast natural materials – the strength of stone with the warmth of wood – to achieve balance. The emphasis is on the structure of the building. Furniture should be simple and decoration sparse so that it takes on an almost sculptural quality, such as a paper-thin porcelain bowl on a stone block in front of a raw plaster wall.

▲ (top) Exposed beams and wooden floors have been stained a rich dark brown. In contrast to the white colour scheme, this creates a fresh, clean look for the bedroom.

▲ (above) From this perspective, the eye is drawn through this all-white decorative scheme to the warm grey colour of the wall in the far room, linked by the muted purple hue of the stair carpet.

▶ Rough plastered walls give this interior an exotic country feel, while the lack of doors and the polished concrete floors give it a modern edge.

new romantic

The New Romantic style has its roots in eighteenth-century French design and formal or classically inspired architecture can form an impressive and complementary framework. High ceilings, panelling, picture rails and elaborate cornices are very much part of the New Romantic look, but that's not to say that it can't also work in other situations where wall treatments will then have a particularly dominant role.

The look is epitomized by the home and work of artist Carolyn Quartermaine. She combines sumptuous silks dyed in vivid shades with ornate but worn gilded furniture and subtle sandstone-coloured walls for a look that is incredibly feminine and rich but also spare, leaving space for the eye to wander and take everything in.

The backdrop for this look is key. If you are fortunate enough to have wood panelling, paint it and any architectural details matt white and combine with natural wood parquet or floorboards. Plaster is left in its natural state, mottled and pinky-beige in colour and decoration is added to walls in a variety of ways. In the kitchen, matt white walls might be covered with old brioche tins arranged haphazardly or in a grid for a vintage take on cladding. Experiment with jelly moulds or hat stays ranged in groups over the walls as an alternative. Elsewhere, sections of walls can be covered with silk for a tactile hit of colour. Choose a traditional moiré pattern for an element of pattern, shot silk to add texture and satin silk to give walls a soft sheeny finish. Use painted wooden beading or a decorative fabric trim to conceal the raw edges. Fragments of architectural plaster moulding, available from salvage yards, can be used to embellish walls; a roundel hung above a bed or a section of a frieze above a marble fireplace is decoration enough.

Flowers are as much a part of this style as the ubiquitous limewashed armoire – fresh and silk flowers and floral prints should be used everywhere. Tie them into long strings using silk

▸ The gilded painting, the deep floating folds of the curtains, the whitewashed walls and the pale and muted colours combine to give this room an ethereal, romantic quality.

▾ (overleaf) The panelling in this apartment is colourwashed with a soft mottled pink and adorned with a decorative gilt mirror and scrolled shelves. The addition of delicate, elegant period furniture and a bed heaped with silk cushions complete the romantic look.

◂ These roughly distressed plaster walls emphasize the look of faded grandeur created by the ornate headboard, embroidered silk bedspread and the curtain with a loose gold motif.

▸ During the process of restoring this house, the remains of this early twentieth-century wallpaper were discovered on the bedroom walls. The owner left the walls intact, decorating it with a perfectly matching Comme des Garçons dress and a string of coral.

ribbon and pin them at intervals along a wall or drape them over picture frames and furniture. Decoupage (see p40) botanical rose prints onto walls in a hallway or small bedroom. First tint the prints with delicate pink and creamy yellow and then finish with an antiquing glaze for a timeworn look. Alternatively, introduce the floral element into a living room by stencilling a single rose motif over one wall. Use fairly strong reds and pinks, then apply a white colourwash or limewash over the entire area, building up the intensity of white in some areas more than others so that it looks as though the rose pattern is shining through several layers of old paint.

As with the Modern Rustic style, there is an aged feel to this look that can be achieved with a variety of paint effects. Use gilding with an antiquing patina (see p31) on furniture, decorative mouldings and woodwork. Crackle-varnish panels in a painted door in patches so that it looks as if the paint has stretched and cracked as the door has aged. Be inspired by the cool tones of the Gustavian period in Scandinavian design and use blue-greys and beige to spatter paint (see p25) on the walls. This will provide an excellent backdrop for ornate furniture with a stained or painted finish. Silver leaf also works well with these colours and can be used to highlight raised plaster details or decorative carving on furniture. Any of the distressed plaster finishes will work well with this look (see pp36–37).

Applying silk paper for a soft textured look (see p39) is a good way of treating plaster walls that are just too old to be left in their natural state. This technique also works with coloured tissue paper, although as the dye in the tissue is not fixed and will bleed as soon as you wet it, you will need to experiment on a piece of board before you start on the wall to make sure you get the desired finish. For a patterned effect, try spattering diluted bleach on the tissue before applying to the walls.

Gilded Picture Frame

This is a simple way of creating a decorative focal point above a fireplace and involves gilding wooden decorative moulding with Dutch aluminium leaf, which is then aged to soften the silver. It could be used to create a rococo-style panel to frame a vintage dress or piece of plasterwork. Experiment with limewashing (see p35) the walls or using crackle varnish (see p30) within the framed area for a timeworn feel.

Many DIY shops now sell various styles of wooden moulding, but for more ornate designs look up specialist plaster suppliers. Plaster moulding can be gilded and aged like wood, and although it is more fragile and usually more expensive, it tends to be more ornate.

Tools & materials

WOOD OR PLASTER MOULDING
WHITE MATT EMULSION
CONTAINER FOR MIXING PAINT
SMALL EMULSION BRUSHES
ACRYLIC SIZE
DUTCH ALUMINIUM METAL LEAF
SOFT-BRISTLED BRUSH
SCALPEL KNIFE
SOFT CLOTHS
ANTIQUING PATINA
ACRYLIC VARNISH AND BRUSH
NAIL-FREE GLUE

Method

1. First mix equal parts of white emulsion and water in a container. Stir well and then paint onto the wood or plaster moulding, taking care to cover all of it. Leave to dry.
2. Stir the acrylic size and paint it onto the moulding in an even coat. Leave to dry for roughly 20 minutes or until the size becomes clear and is still sticky to touch.
3. Carefully lift a sheet of aluminium leaf and lay it on the moulding, gently patting it down with a soft-bristled brush. Collect any flakes that don't adhere to the surface to use for other areas. Remember that some bare patches will help to create the illusion of age.
4. Cut the excess aluminium leaf at the edge of the frame with a scalpel knife.
5. Using a soft cloth, gently rub over the leaf until it is smooth and shiny.
6. Using another soft cloth, gently rub a little antiquing patina into the surface of the moulding, allowing it to build up more in some areas than others. Use it sparingly.
7. Next, apply a thin layer of acrylic varnish to protect the aluminium leaf and bring out the shine. Attach to the wall with nail-free glue.

Tip

▸ Use this technique to create thicker or more ornate borders with plaster mouldings that can be painted or gilded and attached to the wall.

For more information on gilding techniques see p31.

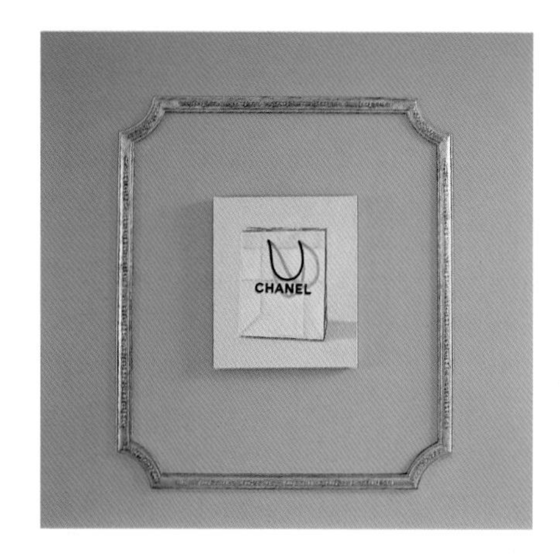

CHANEL

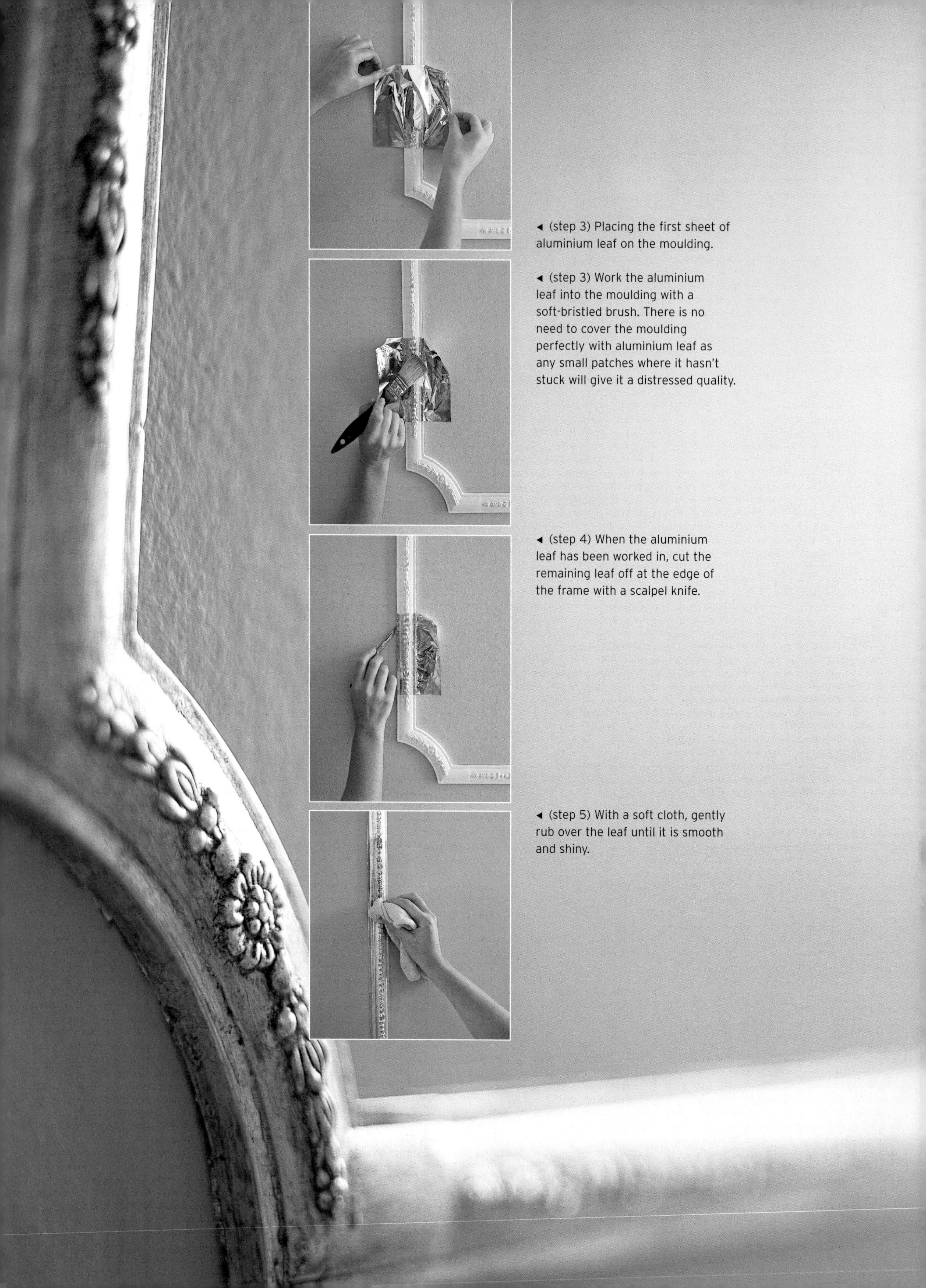

◂ (step 3) Placing the first sheet of aluminium leaf on the moulding.

◂ (step 3) Work the aluminium leaf into the moulding with a soft-bristled brush. There is no need to cover the moulding perfectly with aluminium leaf as any small patches where it hasn't stuck will give it a distressed quality.

◂ (step 4) When the aluminium leaf has been worked in, cut the remaining leaf off at the edge of the frame with a scalpel knife.

◂ (step 5) With a soft cloth, gently rub over the leaf until it is smooth and shiny.

CHANEL

Paints

Annie Sloan
117 London Road
Oxford OX3 9HZ
UK
Tel: +44 (0) 1865 768666
www.anniesloan.com
Pigments, lustres, bronze powders, wax, varnish, brushes and paints

Bailey Paints
Griffin Mill Estate
London Road
New Stroud
Thrupp
Gloucestershire GL5 2AZ
UK
Tel: +44 (0) 1453 882237
www.baileypaints.demon.co.uk
Paints and pigments

Benjamin Moore
USA
Tel: +800 826 2623 for nearest supplier
www.benjaminmoore.com
Paint specialist

L Cornelissen & Son
105 Great Russell Street
London WC1B 3RY
UK
Tel: +44 (0) 20 7636 1045
www.cornelissen.com
Pigments, glazes, metallics and gilding materials

Craig & Rose
Unit 8
Halbeath
Dunfermline
Fife KY11 7EG
UK
Tel: +44 (0) 1383 740000
Range includes glitter, pearlised and metallic paints

Daler Rowney Ltd
Bracknell
Berkshire RG12 8ST
UK
Tel: +44 (0) 1344 424621
www.daler-rowney.com
Artists' acrylic and oil colours

Dulux
UK
Tel: +44 (0) 1753 550555
www.dulux.com
Heritage colours and colour matching service

Dylon International Ltd
Worsley Bridge Road
Lower Sydenham
London SE26 5HD
UK
Tel: +44 (0) 20 8663 4292
www.dylon.co.uk
Dyes

The English Stamp Company
Worth Matravers
Dorset BH19 3JP
UK
Tel: +44 (0) 1929 439117
www.englishstamp.com
Stamps, rollers and paints for use on walls

Farrow & Ball
33 Uddens Trading Estate
Wimborne
Dorset BH21 7NL
UK
Tel: +44 (0) 1202 876141
www.farrow-ball.com
Makes the National Trust range of paints including distemper, dead flat oil, oil eggshell and oil full gloss finishes

Fired Earth
Twyford Mill
Oxford Road
Adderbury
Oxon OX17 3HP
UK
Tel: +44 (0) 1295 812088
www.firedearth.co.uk
Makes the V&A range of historic colours

Francesca's Limewash
Unit 24a
Battersea Business Centre
99/109 Lavender Hill
London SW11 5QL
UK
Tel: +44 (0) 20 7228 7694
Traditional limewash paint

Green & Stone
259 Kings Road
London SW3 5EL
UK
Tel: +44 (0) 20 7352 0837
Artists' supplies

International Ltd
Brewery House
High Street, Twyford
Winchester SO21 1RG
UK
Tel: +44 (0) 1962 717001
Paints for metal, wood and concrete

Modern Masters
7340 Green Bush Avenue
North Hollywood
California 91605
USA
Tel: +1 818 765 2915
Reactive metal paints, patinas, pigment and paints

Paint and Paper Library
5 Elystan Street
London SW3 3NT
UK
Tel: +44 (0) 20 7823 7755

and
Fonthill Ltd
979 Third Avenue
New York
NY 10022
USA
Tel: +1 212 755 6700
www.paintlibrary.co.uk
Handmade paints

Plascon International Ltd
Brewery House
High Street
Twyford
Winchester S021 1RG
UK
Tel: +44 (0) 1962 717001
www.plascon.co.uk
Paints for wood, metal, concrete and brick

Plasti-Kote Ltd
PO Box 867
Pampisford
Cambridge CB2 4XP
UK
Tel: +44 (0) 1223 836686
www.plasti-kote.com
Spray paints including stone flecking and crackle effects

Porter's Original Paints
Sydney
Australia
Tel: +61 18 623 9394
www.porters.com.au

Valspar
US
Tel: +1 800 767 2532 for nearest stockist
www.valspar.com
Glazes and tints

The Wooster Brush Company
Wooster
OH 44691
USA
Tel: +1 800 392 7246
www.woosterbrush.com
Thousands of painting tools including brushes and rollers

Stencils

American Home Stencils
10007 South 76th Street
Franklin W1 53132
USA
Tel: +1 800 742 4520
www.americanhomestencils.com
Stencil brushes, stencils and paints

LA Stencilworks
16115 Vanowen St
Van Nuys
California 91406
USA
Tel: +1 877 989 0262
www.lastencil.com
Large collection of stencils, contemporary designs and mural stencils

Stencil Library
Stocksfield Hall
Stocksfield
Northumberland NE43 7TN
UK
Tel: +44 (0) 1661 844844
www.stencil-library.com
Large range of modern and traditional stencils

Stencil Store
20–21 Heronsgate Road
Chorley Wood
Hertfordshire WD3 5BN
UK
Tel: +44 (0) 1322 427819
www.stencilstore.com

Specialist Finishes

Artex
Pasture Lane
Ruddington
Nottinghamshire NG11 6AG
UK
Tel: +44 (0) 1159 456100
Textural wall finishes

Colron
Ronseal Ltd
Thorncliffe Park
Chapeltown
Sheffield S35 2YP
UK
Tel: +44 (0) 1142 467171
www.ronseal.co.uk
Wood stains, varnish and waxes

Cuprinol
Adderwell
Frome
Somerset BA11 1NL
UK
Tel: +44 (0) 1373 475000
www.cuprinol.co.uk
Wood stains and varnishes

Fine Paints of Europe
PO Box 419
Woodstock
VT 05091
USA
Tel: +1 800 332 1556
www.finepaints.com
Suppliers of Swedish putty and graining rollers

Mylands
John Mylands
80 Norwood High Street
London SE27 9NW
UK
Tel: +44 (0) 20 8670 9161
www.mylands.com
Liming wax and wax

E Ploton Ltd
273 Archway Road
London N6 5AA
UK
Tel: +44 (0) 20 8348 0315
www.ploton.co.uk
Specialist materials including brushes, gilding supplies, wood graining tools and glazes

Polyvine Ltd
Marybrook Street, Berkeley
Gloucestershire GL13 9AA
UK
Tel: 0870 787 3710
USA tel: +1 661 775 1919
www.polyvine.com
Specialist brushes, waxes, stains and colourisers

Wallcoverings

Alma Home
12–14 Greatorex St
London E1 5NF
UK
Tel: +44 (0) 20 7377 0762
www.almahome.co.uk
Leather and suede wall tiles

Aristocast Originals
49a Ogreave Close
Doorhouse Industrial Estate
Hansworth
Sheffield S13 9NP
UK
Tel: +44 (0) 114 269 0900
Original feature plasterwork

Atelier Corozo
ZI de la Croix Saint Georges
16500 Confolens
France
Tel: +33 545 85 43 22
Reproduction antique frescoes

The Cane Store
207 Blackstock Road
London N5 2LL
UK
Tel: +44 (0) 20 7354 4210
www.canestore.co.uk
Bamboo, cane, woven cane, seagrass, rush, raffia and willow

Chauncey's
16 Feeder Road
Bristol BS2 0SB
UK
Tel: +44 (0) 1179 713131
Panelling

Copley Decor Ltd
Leyburn
North Yorkshire DL8 5QA
UK
Tel: +44 (0) 1969 623410
www.copleydecor.co.uk
Architectural mouldings made from resin

Crown Berger Ltd
PO Box 37
Crown House, Hollins Road
Darwen
Lancashire BB3 0BG
UK
Tel: +44 (0) 1254 704951
www.crownpaint.co.uk
Anaglypta paints, relief wallcoverings

Deacon & Sandys
Hillcrest Farm Oast
Hawkhurst Road
Cranbrook
Kent TN17 3QD
UK
Tel: +44 (0) 1580 713775

Décor Shades
5 Brewery Mews Business Centre
St John's Road
Isleworth
Middlesex TW7 6PH
UK
Tel: +44 (0) 20 8847 1939
Paper backing of fabrics for wallcoverings

Dryvit Systems Inc
One Energy Way
West Warwick
RI 02893
USA
Tel: +1 800 556 7752
UK tel: 44 (0) 1462 819555
www.dryvit.com
Stucco

Emmerique Isabelle
5 rue Bouin
92700 Colombes
France
Tel: +33 147 86 09 49
Lacquered wall panels

Hallidays
The Old Cottage
Dorchester-on-Thames
Oxfordshire OX10 7HL
UK
Tel: +44 (0) 1865 340068
www.hallidays.com
Georgian panelling and fireplaces

CF Handerson
36 Graham Street
London N1 8JX
UK
Tel: +44 (0) 20 7226 1212
Supplies beech, cherry and oak veneered boards for wall panelling

Heritage Oak
Unit V5
Dean Clough Industrial Park
Halifax
West Yorkshire HX3 5AX
UK
Tel: +44 (0) 1422 348231
Restoration work, panelling and wainscots

Hosek Manufacturing Company
4877 National Western Drive
Denver
CO 80216
USA
Architectural mouldings

Howard Chairs
30–31 Lyme Street
London NW1 0EE
UK
Tel: +44 (0) 20 7482 2156
Backing of fabric for wallcoverings

Jali
Apsley House, Chartham
Kent CT4 7HT
UK
Tel: +44 (0) 1227 831710
www.jali.co.uk
Mdf decorative fretwork, trims and trellis

Tracey Kendall
116 Greyhound Lane
London SW16 5RN
UK
Tel: +44 (0) 20 8769 0618
Bespoke papers, banners and stitched papers

EW Moore
39 Plashet Grove
London E6 1AD
UK
Tel: +44 (0) 20 8471 9392
Large-scale photo murals

Kate Osborn
UK tel: +44 (0) 20 7727 0949
Large-scale photographic images

Ornamenta
3/12 Chelsea Harbour Design Centre
London SW10 0XE
UK
Tel: +44 (0) 20 7352 1824
www.ornamenta.co.uk
Site-specific papers

Victorian Woodworks
International House
London International Freight Terminal
Temple Mills Lane
Stratford
London E15 2ES
UK
Tel: +44 (0) 20 8534 1000
www.victorianwoodworks.com
Bead and buckwood panelling

Wallpapers

Agnes Bourne
2 Henry Adams Street
220 San Francsico
CA 94103
USA

Andrew Martin
200 Walton Street
London SW3 2JL
UK
Tel: +44 (0) 20 7584 4290

Anna French
343 Kings Road
London SW3 5ES
UK
Tel: +44 (0) 20 7351 1126

Avant Garde Designs Ltd
Shop 133, The Mall
Pacific Place 2
88 Queensway
Hong Kong
Tel: +852 2840 1627

Bradbury & Bradbury Art Wallpapers
PO Box 155
Benicia
CA 94510
USA
Tel: +1 707 746 1900
www.bradbury.com

Brunschwig & Fils
979 Third Avenue
12th Floor
New York
NY 10022 1234
USA
Tel: +1 212 838 7878

and
10 The Chambers
Chelsea Harbour Drive
London SW10 0XF
UK
Tel: +44 (0) 20 7351 5797
www.brunschwig.com

C&A Wallcoverings
23745 Mercantile Rd
Cleveland
OH 44122
USA
Tel: +1 216 464 3700

Cath Kidston Limited
8 Clarendon Cross
London W11 4PE
UK
Tel: +44 (0) 20 7221 4000
www.cathkidston.co.uk
1950s retro designs

Cole & Son Wallpapers
G10 Chelsea Harbour Design Centre
London SW10 0XE
UK
Tel: +44 (0) 20 7376 4623
www.cole-and-son.com
Specialize in flock wallpaper

Colefax & Fowler
110 Fulham Rd
London SW3 6RL
UK
Tel: +44 (0) 20 7244 7427

Creative Wallcovering
403 South Riverdale Drive
Durham NC 27712
USA
Tel: +1 800 342 6113
www.creativewallcovering.com
An online catalogue of wallcoverings, wall murals and wallpaper borders for children

Designers Guild
275–7 Kings Rd
London SW3 5EN
UK
Tel: +44 (0) 20 7243 7300

and
Einrichtuings GMBH
Dreimuhlenstrasse 38A
80469 Munich
Germany
Tel: +49 89 2311 620

and
10 rue Saint Nicolas
75012 Paris
France
Tel: +33 44 67 80 70
www.designersguild.com

Eisenhart Wallcoverings Co
PO Box 464
Hanover
PA 17331
Germany
Tel: +1 800 931 9255
www.eisenwalls.com

Jane Churchill
151 Sloane Street
London SW1X 9BZ
UK
Tel: +44 (0) 20 7730 9847

Neisha Crosland
137 Fulham Rd
London SW3 6DS
UK
Tel: +44 (0) 20 7978 4389

and
16 West 55th Street
Suite 1R
New York
NY 10019
USA
Tel: +1 212 397 8257

Noblis
29 rue Bonaparte
75006 Paris
France
Tel: +33 (0) 143 29 21 50
www.nobilis.fr

Ornamenta
(see address in wallcoverings)

Osborne & Little
304–8 Kings Road
London SW3 5UH
UK
Tel: +44 (0) 20 8675 2255
www.osborneandlittle.com

Paint and Paper Library
(see address in paints)

Sanderson
Sanderson House
Oxford Road
Denham UB9 4DX
UK
Tel: +44 (0) 1895 830000

and
233 Kings Road
London SW3 5EJ
UK
Tel: +44 (0) 20 7351 7728
www.sanderson-online.co.uk

Stroheim & Romann
31–11 Thomson Ave
Long Island City
NY 11101
USA
Tel: +1 718 706 7000
www.stroheim.com

Timorous Beasties
7 Craigend Place
Glasgow
Scotland G13 2UN
UK
Tel: +44 (0) 141 959 3331
www.timorousbeasties.com
Fabrics, wallcoverings and accessories

Tapi
Kommendorsgatan 22
114 48 Stockholm
Sweden
Tel: +46 8 661 0380

USA Wallpaper
129 Columbus Avenue
Sandusky OH 44870
USA
Tel: +1 800 573 5824
www.usawallpaper.com

Usera Usera
Ayala 56
28001 Madrid
Spain
Tel: +34 91 577 9461

Victoria Schoeller-Szuts
Boersegasse 9 and 10
A-1010 Vienna
Austria
Tel: +43 1535 3075

Wardlaw PTY Ltd
230–232 Auburn Rd
Hawthorn Melbourne
Victoria 3122
Australia
Tel: +613 9819 4233

Waverly
79 Madison Avenue
New York
NY 10016
USA
Tel: + 1 718 392 3999
www.waverly.com
Fabrics, wallcoverings and wallpapers

Zuber & Cie
5 boulevard des Filles du Calvaire
75003 Paris
France
Tel: +33 1 42 77 95 91

and
D&D Building
979 Third Avenue
New York
NY 10022
USA
Tel: +1 212 486 9226

and
42 Pimlico Road
London SW1W 8LP
UK
Tel: +44 (0) 20 7824 8265
www.zuber.fr
Handpainted wallpapers and fabrics

Page numbers in *italics* refer to captions.

index

Publisher's Acknowledgements

The publisher would like to thank the following photographers and agencies for their kind permission to reproduce the photographs in this book:

5 below left Herbert Ypma/The Interior Archive; 5 below right Verne Fotografie; 7 Vitlycke Museum, Tanum, Bohuslan, Sweden/Bridgeman Art Library; 8 above J. March Penney/Camera Press; 8 below National Museum of India, New Delhi, India/Bridgeman Art Library; 9 Musee de l'Oeuvre de Notre Dame, Strasbourg, France/Bridgeman Art Library; 10 above Mark Fiennes/Loseley Park, Guildford, UK/Bridgeman Art Library; 10 below Palazzo del Quirinale, Rome, Italy/Bridgeman Art Library; 11 Angelo Hornak Library; 12 above Villa Marcello, Veneto, Italy/Bridgeman Art Library; 12 below Grand Duke Nicholas's Palace, St. Petersburg, Russia/Bridgeman Art Library; 13 Osterley Park, UK/Bridgeman Art Library; 14 above Angelo Hornak Library (Courtesy of The Royal Pavilion, Brighton); 14 below Ray Main/Mainstream; 15 Ray Main/Mainstream (Eltham Palace); 16 Richard Bryant/Arcaid (Architect: Edward Ould); 17 above & below Bridgeman Art Library; 18 Angelo Hornak Library; 19 Nathalie Krag (Stylist: Tami Christiansen); 22, 44-45 & 46 above Ray Main/Mainstream; 46 below right John Mason/*Homes & Gardens*/ipc magazines; 47 Simon Upton/The Interior Archive (Designer: Lars Sjoeberg); 49 Ray Main/Mainstream; 50-51 Designed by Jane Gordon Clark for Ornamenta; 52 Nick Pope/*Living Etc*/ipc magazines; 53 Ray Main/Mainstream (Flying Duck Enterprises); 56 Ray Main/Mainstream; 57 Hotze Eisma/VT Wonen/Sanoma Syndication; 58 above right M. Grazia Branco/Ikebranco; 58 below left Paul Raeside/*Living Etc*/ipc magazines; 59 Paul Ryan/International Interiors (Carl Linnaeus, Hammerby); 60-61 Debi Treloar/*Homes & Gardens*/ipc magazines; 62 Craig Knowles/*Elle Decoration* (Stylist: Finola Inger; Design: The Stencil Library); 63 & 68 Caroline Arber/*Homes & Gardens*/ipc magazines; 69 Torsten Oelscher/*Elle Decoration* (Stylist: Amanda Smith); 70-71 Pia Tryde (Courtesy of Cath Kidston); 72-73 Erin Haydn O'Neill/House of Pictures; 74 above left Giorgio Possenti/Vega MG; 74 above right & 74 below right Ray Main/Mainstream; 75 Graham Atkins-Hughes/*Elle Decoration* (Stylist: Jenny Dalton; Architect: Project Orange); 76 & 77 Ray Main/Mainstream; 80-81 Ray Main/Mainstream (Design: Filer & Cox); 82 Nick Hufton/View (Architect: Mathias Klotz); 83 Verne Fotografie (Architect: Inge Watteeuw); 84 above Ray Main/Mainstream; 84 below Marcus Wilson-Smith; 85 Giorgio Possenti/Vega MG; 86 left Gianni Basso/Vega MG; 86 right Christopher Drake/*Homes & Gardens*/ipc magazines; 87 Giorgio Possenti/Vega MG; 88 left Doreen Dierckx; 88 right & 89 Verne Fotografie; 90 above Ray Main/Mainstream; 90 below Mark Luscombe-Whyte/The Interior Archive (Architect: Le Corbusier); 91 Verne Fotografie (Inge Watteeuw); 92 Camera Press; 93 above & 93 below Verne Fotografie; 94-95, 101 & 102 Ray Main/Mainstream; 103 Mark Williams/Red Cover; 104 Ray Main/Mainstream; 105 Verne Fotografie (Architect: Ettore Sottsass); 106-107 Marc Broussard (Stylist: Catherine Taralon/Design: Francoise de Pfyffer); 108 above Damian Russell/*Elle Decoration* (Stylist: Amanda Smith); 108 below Verne Fotografie (Architect: Axel Ghyssaert, Brugge); 109 Jan Baldwin/Narratives; 110 above Ray Main/Mainstream; 110 below Simon Upton/The Interior Archive (Designer: Dolce & Gabbana); 111 Neil Mersh/*Elle Decoration* (Stylist: Amanda Smith); 116-117 Mark Luscombe-Whyte/The Interior Archive (Architect: Le Corbusier); 118 Paul Ryan/International Interiors (Designer: Wolfgang Joop); 119 M. Grazia Branco/Ikebranco; 121 Simon Upton/The Interior Archive (Designer: Carolyn Quartermaine); 122 Simon Upton/The Interior Archive (Designer: Hable & Smith); 123 left Verne Fotografie; 128 Caroline Arber/*Homes & Gardens*/ipc magazines; 129 Dennis Brandsma/VT Wonen/Sanoma Syndication; 130 above Andreas von Einsiedel (Interior Designer: David Collins); 130 below Verne Fotografie; 131 John Dummer/Taverne Agency (Designer: Karin Draaijer); 135 Mikkel Vang/Taverne Agency (Production: Christine Rudolph); 136 above Jan Verlinde; 136 below Giulio Oriani/Vega MG (Casa Claudio Zambrano); 137 & 138 above Amparo Garrido/Album; 138 below Giulio Oriani/Vega MG; 139 Verne Fotografie; 144 Mark Luscombe-Whyte/The Interior Archive (Designer: Kurt Bredenbeck); 145 Jose van Riele/*Marie Claire Maison* (Stylist: Carin Scheve); 146 above & below, 147 Verne Fotografie; 148 above Jose van Riele/*Marie Claire Maison* (Stylist: D. Rozenstroch); 148 below Giorgio Possenti/Vega MG; 149 Gianni Basso/Vega MG; 150-151 Marc Broussard (Design: Roberto Bergero); 152 Verne Fotografie; 153 Guilio Oriani/Vega MG; 154 Steve Jones/Axiom Photographic Agency; 155 Eric Morin/*Elle Decoration* (Owner: Shaun Clarkson); 156 Jose van Riele/*Marie Claire Maison* (Production: D. Rozensztroch); 157 Gilles de Chabaneix/*Marie Claire Idées* (Stylist: Catherine de Chabaneix); 158 above Jan Baldwin/Narratives; 158 below Neil Barclay/Axiom Photographic Agency; 159 Jan Baldwin/Narratives; 160 Rolant Dafis; 161 Luuk Geertsen/VT Wonen/Sanoma Syndication; 162 Doreen Dierckx; 163 James Mitchell/Red Cover; 168 above Verne Fotografie; 168 below Jan Baldwin/Narratives (Langlands & Bell); 169 Simon Upton/The Interior Archive (Designer: Lars Sjoeberg); 170-171 Mirjam Bleeker/Taverne Agency (Production: Jet Krings); 172 above Christopher Drake/Red Cover; 172 below & 173 Verne Fotografie; 175 Solvi Dos Santos (Owner: Anna Bonde); 176-177 Ingalill Snitt/Agence Snitt; 178 Simon Upton/The Interior Archive (Designer: Carolyn Quartermaine); 179 Andrea Ferrari (Owner: Isabella Sodi).

Every effort has been made to trace the copyright holders and we apologise in advance for any unintentional omission and would be pleased to insert the appropriate acknowledgement in any subsequent edition.

With many thanks to the following organisations for providing the props for photography:

The Conran Shop (contemporary furniture, furnishings and accessories) Michelin House, 81 Fulham Road, London SW3 6RD, telephone 020 7591 8702, www.conran.com; **Heal's** (contemporary furniture, furnishings & accessories) The Heal's Building, 196 Tottenham Court Road, London W1A 1BJ, telephone 020 7636 1666, www.heals.co.uk; **Habitat** (contemporary furniture & accessories) The Heal's Building, 196 Tottenham Court Road, London W1A 1BJ, telephone 0845 6010740, www.habitat.net; **IKEA** (Swedish superstore with economical furniture & accessories) telephone 020 8208 5600 for branches, www.ikea.com; **M.C. Stone** (bathroom and flooring design) 69A Goldney Road, London W9 2AR, telephone 020 7266 3644, www.mcstone.co.uk; **Laura Ashley** (traditional fabrics, paints, tiles, wallcoverings, furniture & accessories) telephone 01686 622116 for branches, www.laura-ashley.com; **Vessel** (contemporary sculptural glassware, ceramics and china) 114 Kensington Park Road, London W11 2PW; **Brian Ayling** (contemporary art by commission) telephone 020 8802 9853.

The publisher would also like to thank Anne-Marie Hoines for her assistance with the picture research.

Author's Acknowledgements

I would like to thank all the talented people without whom this book would not exist: the team at Conran Octopus, especially Emma Clegg, Lucy Gowans and Rachel Davies; Muna and Carl for getting the project off the ground; Chris Tubbs for beautiful pictures; Sara Emslie for fantastic styling; Sascha Cohen for paint-effect swatches; Andy Knight for brilliant set building; Keith and Elma for years of encouragement and support; and Andy for his patience and for always being there.